build a better burger

Celebrating Sutter Home's Annual Search
for America's Best Burgers

James McNair

**Food Photography by
Noel Barnhurst**

TEN SPEED PRESS
Berkeley | Toronto

Ten Speed Press
Box 7123
Berkeley, California 94707
www.tenspeed.com

Distributed in Australia by Simon & Schuster Australia, in Canada by Ten Speed Press Canada, in New Zealand by Southern Publishers Group, in South Africa by Real Books, and in the United Kingdom and Europe by Airlift Book Company.

Project direction by James McNair
Design direction by Andrew Rice
Editorial direction by Aaron Wehner

Design by Jennifer Barry Design, Fairfax, California
Layout production by Kristen Wurz

Text by James McNair
Editorial assistance by Andrew Moore
Burger and wine pairing by Jeffrey Starr
Edited by Holly Taines White
Copyedited by Marchelle Brain

Food photography by Noel Barnhurst, San Francisco
Photography assistance by Noriko Akiyama, Gene Lee, and Sara Johnson Loehmann
Food styling by Sandra Cook
Styling assistance by Elisabet der Nederlanden and Penny Zweidinger
Contest photography by M. J. Wickham, unless noted otherwise on page 200
Front cover photography (left and center): Getty Images
Additional photography credits on page 200

Library of Congress Cataloging-in-Publication Data
McNair, James K.
Build a better burger : celebrating Sutter Home's annual
search for America's best burgers / James McNair.
p. cm.
Includes index.
Summary: "A collection of winners' and judges' recipes from the annual
Sutter Home Vineyards Build a Better Burger contest, including more than
50 unique burgers"—Provided by publisher.
ISBN-10: 1-58008-720-5 (pbk.)
ISBN-13: 978-1-58008-720-9 (pbk.)
1. Hamburgers. I. Sutter Home Family Vineyards. II. Title.
TX749.5.B43M375 2005
641.8'4—dc22   2004029244

Printed in Thailand

1 2 3 4 5 6 7 8 9 10 — 09 08 07 06 05

contents

Acknowledgments

I'd like to raise a glass of Sutter Home wine to toast the following for helping make this book a reality. Cheers and thanks to each one!

To the Trinchero family, owners of Sutter Home, for supporting the Build a Better Burger competition throughout its history.

To the founding cook-off team: the late Alex Morgan, Sutter Home's first marketing director, and Stan Hock, former winery communications director, for developing the idea and inviting me to judge the first cook-off.

To Mary Ann Vangrin, senior director of public relations at Sutter Home; Wendy Nyberg, senior director of marketing; and Terry Wheatley, vice president of marketing, for guiding BBB as it's grown bigger and better each year, and for commissioning and nurturing this book project. And to Bob Torkelson, president of Sutter Home, for his strong support of the cook-off.

To Jeffrey Starr, Sutter Home's star chef, for contributing the wine recommendations for each recipe and great tips for pairing wine with burgers.

To the past and present staff of Sutter Home, for their extremely hard work to stage the annual cook-off, especially to Michele Moline, event manager extraordinaire.

To Andrew Moore, my partner, for his abiding support, his enthusiastic assistance in every aspect of my work on Build a Better Burger, and for his invaluable help on this volume.

To Lorena Jones, publisher at Ten Speed Press, and Aaron Wehner, editorial director, for eagerly taking on this project and overseeing its production so competently. And to Holly Taines White, editor, for her gentle guidance and proficiency, and Marchelle Brain, copyeditor, for skillfully honing the text.

To Andrew Rice, director of design at Sutter Home, for putting together the design and photography team and offering his creative ideas.

To Jennifer Barry, design visionaire, and her assistant Kristen Wurz for turning my words and ideas into a beautiful book.

To Sandra Cook, food stylist, and her assistants Elisabet der Nederlanden and Penny Zweidinger for making each burger look so appealing.

To Noel Barnhurst, photographer, and his assistants Noriko Akiyama, Sara Johnson Loehmann, and Gene Lee for capturing the images of the burgers so artfully.

To M. J. Wickham, location and event photographer, for archiving so many of the cook-offs with her unique and casual style.

To my fellow food professionals who've given of their time to journey to Napa Valley to join me in judging the national cook-off. And a big thanks to those who contributed their favorite burger recipes for this book.

To all the entrants of Build a Better Burger, for the many thousands of creative recipes submitted over the past fifteen years. And to all the finalists and winners of the cook-offs for the hundreds of better burgers I've tasted. You've made my summers challenging and fun!

Foreword

More than fifty years ago, my father, Mario, and mother, Mary, moved our family from a comfortable apartment in bustling midtown Manhattan to what was at the time a sleepy farming community called Napa Valley. My father wanted to give his children a life in the countryside, which reminded him of his home back in Italy. He and his brother had purchased a historic winery shuttered since Prohibition called Sutter Home. And he enlisted the help of his entire family to build a winery business, including my sister, Vera, our brother, Roger, and my beautiful wife, Evalyn. Eventually, Vera's sons, Tony and Bobby, joined the crew, and we're proud to be family owned and operated to this day.

For many years, we operated Sutter Home as essentially a mom-and-pop winery. Eventually, I became winemaker, and a serious one at that. My passion was Zinfandel—the red kind. In an attempt to make the biggest, boldest, richest Zinfandel possible, I happened to stumble on a little wine we called White Zinfandel. That wine changed all of our lives forever. It was a wine that people could enjoy every day, with all kinds of food. Not serious—just delicious.

Fifteen years ago, we wanted to assure Americans, who seemed more likely to enjoy beer and soda pop with casual meals, that it was okay to go a little crazy and have a glass of wine with, say, a big, juicy hamburger. There wasn't any reason to wait for the white tablecloth or the special occasion. Our Italian heritage taught us that wine was created to be enjoyed with food—all kinds of food. We thought America should know that.

So in 1991, we created the Build a Better Burger National Recipe Contest and Cook-Off®. It was a great way to promote our food and wine philosophy—and to sell a few extra cases of wine during the summer months, typically a slow wine season. In the ensuing years, we have received thousands and thousands of stunning burger recipes using every

ingredient you can imagine. These burgers draw on dozens of different culinary traditions, using flavors and ingredients from around the world. For me, they bring the idea of America as a melting pot to life. And, needless to say, I have enjoyed myself thoroughly over the years sampling the finalists' recipes and helping to select the winners on several occasions. My brother has also judged the competition a couple of times and our sister has never missed a cook-off.

I am thrilled to be part of this book and the fifteenth anniversary celebration of Build a Better Burger. We've come a long way over the years, and I'm happy to say more Americans are enjoying wine than ever before—just like the Italians—over a simple meal, on a regular day, with family and friends. So browse through the recipes, fire up your grill, and build yourself a better burger. They're all winners. And, by the way, as far as the wine is concerned—put it in any glass you like! Buon appetito!

—Bob Trinchero, Chairman, Trinchero Family Estates

Celebrating Better Burgers

a s patties sizzling on hot grills exude their seductive aromas, Sutter Home Family Vineyards' annual nationwide search for the best burger comes to another rip-roaring conclusion at the Build a Better Burger National Cook-Off. Carefully chosen contestants converge each year on a sun-drenched, early autumn Saturday in St. Helena, California, to prepare their unique burgers for judging by a group of highly qualified chefs, culinary journalists, food magazine editors, cookbook authors, and other luminaries of the professional food world. While everyone eagerly awaits the results, cook-off guests gather beneath a big tent to watch the proceedings, sample burgers and innovative side dishes, sip **Sutter Home** wines, and enjoy lively music from a popular band.

Earlier in the year, the annual Build a Better Burger contest kicks off on Memorial Day weekend, the unofficial start of grilling season. Entries begin trickling in at first and pick up speed during July until the final avalanche arrives shortly before Labor Day. Each entry is carefully screened to make certain that it conforms to the requirements of the contest. Sadly, more than half of the entries are quickly disqualified for failing to follow the rules. Then the qualified recipes are carefully scrutinized and the most appealing go into the Better Burgers file.

Throughout the summer, the **best recipes** are periodically reevaluated and narrowed down. During Labor Day weekend, these are whittled down to a small handful of top favorites in each region. Those burgers are then cooked to determine the finalists from each region.

The finalists are flown to **Napa Valley** to compete head to head in the heated cook-off.

The exciting cook-off weekend gets under way on Friday, when the creative finalists and their companions from every region of the country arrive in Napa Valley. After checking into the Sutter Home Inn on the outskirts of the charming town of St. Helena, they while away the afternoon meeting and greeting their competition, hearing the final details of the adventure that lies ahead, and checking the ingredients and utensils that will be used at their cooking stations. That evening, they are wined and dined at a leisurely dinner, usually prepared by Sutter Home chef Jeffrey Starr and his talented culinary team.

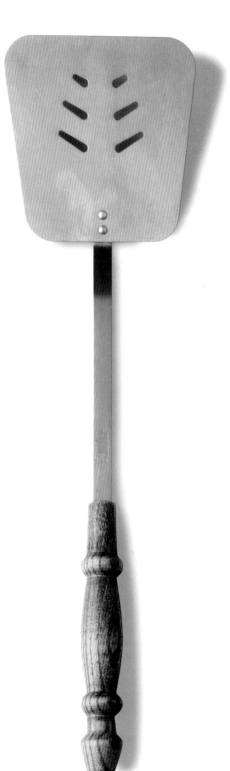

During the early years of **Build a Better Burger,** known colloquially as BBB, the finalists rose early on the cook-off day to shop at a St. Helena supermarket for the ingredients needed to make their burgers. Now, the Sutter Home culinary center staff shops ahead for them, carefully following the ingredient list in each recipe and has everything assembled in individual boxes for the contestants to inspect on Friday afternoon. If anything is not up to a finalist's expectations, the winery staff does its best to accommodate his or her wishes.

The 2002 Grand Prize winner, Annelle Williams, recalls her excitement upon seeing her box of ingredients: "I was overwhelmed, because in my box were beautiful mozzarella and a big chunk of fresh Parmesan, tomatoes that were at the peak of flavor, a bunch of fresh basil with leaves that were perfect for my burger. They were the best of the **best ingredients**, ensuring that our concoctions would be the best they could possibly be for the competition. I couldn't wait to take my groceries and try to convert them into something really **delicious**. The next morning, the chef delivered freshly baked focaccia for the 'bun' part of my recipe. I couldn't

believe how dedicated they were to providing us with such incredible ingredients."

The rules of the cook-off allow finalists to bring along from home any special ingredient or utensil that they wish, and while most are content to leave the shopping to the Sutter Home staff, some have arrived with pita breads from a favorite bakery, handpicked apples from their orchard, or their grandmother's cast-iron skillet in hand.

After a hearty breakfast at the Sutter Home Inn on Saturday morning, the finalists head to their cooking stations at nine in the morning to prepare for the judging, which begins when the first burger is due off the grill at high noon. For the three years that the cook-off was open to the public as a fundraiser, the event was held at the Trinchero's Zinfandel Ranch in the heart of Napa Valley. All other cook-offs have been staged in the lush gardens of the Sutter Home Victorian, a Napa Valley landmark since 1884, where grills are arranged under individual white awnings that shelter each finalist from the hot sun. As the heat of the day rises, so do the **tantalizing aromas** of grilling burgers.

The cook-off is timed so that every few minutes, a finalist presents his or her finished burgers to the judges. Finalists are not allowed to decorate or garnish the plain serving trays, or to offer any side dishes; everything must be between the bun halves or bread slices. Each judge marks a scorecard, without conferring with other members of the panel. For many years, the burgers were scored in three categories: originality of the recipe, ease of preparation, and taste. To make it easier on the judges and get a clearer winner, the procedure now allows each judge to score each burger on a simple Olympics-style system of 1 to 10, keeping in mind the **creativity** involved, the visual appeal of the finished burger, and, most important, the **taste**. After scoring all of the burgers, the votes are counted by a

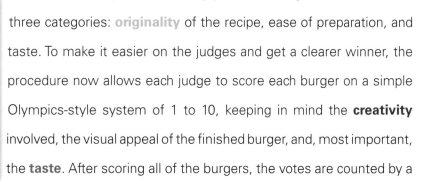

separate tally team, with the judges remaining nearby in case we need to break a tie. (By the way, a lot of people have asked me how we judges cleanse our palates to be able to taste so many different burgers. Watermelon does a terrific job, so the judging station has a big platter of watermelon bites for this purpose.)

what's in the patty?

Look for these symbols under the title of each recipe

Beef

Pork

Buffalo

Lamb

Poultry

Seafood

Veggies

After the finalists and judges have completed their tasks, everyone joins in the party, visiting with the guests and enjoying the music until the awards ceremony. As no contact between contestants and judges has been allowed up to this point, now everyone can meet and chat with each other. At midafternoon, the judges and finalists are introduced to the crowd and the results are announced, with a super-sized check and whimsical ceramic trophy by wine-country sculptress Cynthia Hipkiss presented to the winner of the Grand Prize for the **year's best burger**.

In the Winning Recipes section, you'll find a chronological listing of all recipes that have won cook-off prizes. In the early years, a check for $10,000 was given to each **Grand Prize winner**, with prizes awarded in diminishing amounts to the top runners-up and a special award presented for creativity. Beginning in 1999, these rank-placement and creativity prizes were discontinued and each finalist was awarded a prize of $500. For the new century, the Grand Prize was raised to $20,000 in 2000, and in 2004, it soared to **$50,000**.

Build a Better Burger rules identify a burger as consisting of any food product that can be ground, formed into patties, grilled, and served on or between a bakery product, with any added condiments

or toppings. **Anything goes**, and BBB has seen it all, from the truly bizarre to fabulous innovations. Since the beginnings of the contest, the entries have reflected trends in American cooking. Looking back through the years, it's easy to trace the popularity and general acceptance of food products, beginning with pesto, aioli, and sun-dried tomatoes of the early 1990s, then on to a period of cilantro, ginger, and other Asian flavors, and most recently, the near-obsession with mango and chipotle chiles.

A complete list of all BBB prizewinners and other finalists can be found on pages 194–99. The majority have been "contesters," a highly **creative group of home cooks** who regularly enter cooking competitions and who keep up with the contesting world and each other via Cooking Contest Central (www.contestcooking.com). Many of these "contesters" lavish praise upon BBB because it is one of the few contests where they get a chance to show real culinary skill in their recipes. While most other competitions either require the use of the sponsor's convenience products or limit the number of ingredients, the **sky is the limit** at BBB. One of BBB's Grand Prize winners, Kurt Wait, was an occasional contester who went on to become the first man to win the Pillsbury Bake-Off's® semiannual million-dollar purse.

Although most cooking contests do not allow food professionals to enter, Build a Better Burger does not discriminate, and for one year only, we even singled out the professionals for a separate division. Although we've had chefs and caterers as finalists a number of times, each Grand Prize winner has been an amateur cook. One winner, Porter Lansing, was inspired by his **success at BBB** to train and become a professional chef.

As you will see from the winning recipes, they each reflect creativity and individuality to **achieve the perfect burger**. In addition to recipes from the contestants, we thought that it would be interesting to put the judges to the test, so we turned to some of the well-known food professionals who have participated in the difficult yet fun task of judging the competition to provide a favorite burger recipe. The results prove that no two cooks, even the pros, think alike when it comes to building the perfect burger.

The folks at Sutter Home and Build a Better Burger hope that this volume, like our contest, will **inspire good backyard cooks everywhere** to create better burgers and to share them with the rest of us through this exciting annual competition!

The American Burger

german immigrants from Hamburg brought their city's love of cooked ground beef to American shores in the early 1800s, and it came to be known as "steak cooked in the Hamburg style." A surviving 1834 menu from Delmonico's in New York listed "Hamburger Steak" as a daily offering, and at 10 cents, it was one of the costliest items on the menu. The first published recipe for hamburger steak was in Fanny Farmer's *Boston Cooking School Cook Book* of 1896.

But a hamburger steak is still a bun and a few condiments short of being a burger.

Several families and towns in various locations claim credit for inventing the hamburger, but we'll probably never know for certain who placed the first patty between slices of bread. Yet food historians are in general agreement that it was introduced to the general public in 1904 at the St. Louis World's Fair (officially known as the Louisiana Purchase Exposition).

Writing in the *New York Tribune* from the 1904 fair, a reporter described a new sandwich called a hamburger as "the innovation of a food vendor on the pike [midway]." Historical research indicates that the unnamed concessionaire in the *Tribune* story was most likely Fletcher Davis of Athens, Texas. Known in Athens as "Old Dave," even though he was a fairly young man, Davis began serving an unnamed sandwich at his lunch counter in the late 1880s. His creation consisted of a hamburger steak placed between slices of

warm, home-baked bread that was spread with a mixture of ground mustard and mayonnaise and topped with sliced Bermuda onion and cucumber pickles.

Following the St. Louis fair, the new sandwich spread quickly throughout America, popularized at the portable lunch wagons and carts, diners, soda fountains, luncheonettes, and greasy spoons that popped up everywhere to serve the nation's rapidly expanding workforce.

In 1916 in Wichita, Kansas, J. Walter Anderson flattened the traditional hamburger steak that had been served in the sandwich into a thinner patty that could be cooked quickly. He also created a one-piece bun to substitute for the bread slices commonly in use. From his converted–trolley car diner, Anderson sold small, square burgers for a nickel each and encouraged customers to "buy 'em by the sack." By 1921, his operation had grown to five locations and was renamed "White Castle." This became America's first hamburger chain, offering a standardized look, menu, and service. White Castle pioneered the use of advertising to sell hamburgers and originated the disposable paper hat for food servers.

Like most American success stories, White Castle's triumph spawned numerous imitators, including White Clocks, White Diamonds, White Domes, White Huts, White Manas, White Towers, Royal Castles, and King's Castles, and the fast-food hamburger craze was off and running.

The Pig Stand, America's first drive-in restaurant, opened in Dallas in 1921 and introduced "carhop" service, a term derived from the practice of servers hopping onto the auto running boards to take orders before delivering orders on trays that hung over the windows.

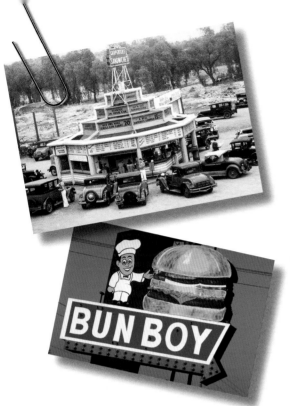

The earliest cheeseburger was probably made in 1924 at the Rite Spot drive-in in Pasadena, California.

The first use of the shortened term "burger" for the hamburger was likely due to J. Wellington Wimpy, who debuted in the *Popeye* comic strips in 1929 and bargained that he "would gladly pay you Tuesday for a hamburger today." The hamburger-loving character became so popular that his favorite sandwiches became known as "Wimpy Burgers."

During the 1930s, streamlined drive-ins with large overhangs to protect the carhops were perfected in California, and in 1934, Steak and Shake carried the drive-in concept to the East Coast.

In 1937, Bob Wian created the first double-decker burger at his lunch counter in Glendale, California, naming it and his restaurant "Big Boy" after a rather large lad who cleaned the restaurant in exchange for burgers. Bob soon became the first hamburger-franchising mogul.

In 1937, brothers Richard and Maurice McDonald opened a little drive-in in Arcadia, California, that would change the world of hamburgers forever, and in 1948, the brothers eliminated carhop service, dishes, glasses, flatware, and their varied cooked-to-order menu and converted their drive-in into the world's first self-service burger bar. The new concept offered only prepackaged burgers with no condiment choices and with ready-cooked fries and drinks in a hurry.

The year 1948 also saw the opening of the first drive-through burger stand—In-N-Out Burger in Baldwin Park, California—eliminating the need for patrons to get out of their cars to order and pick up their burgers.

In 1949, Googies in Los Angeles introduced modernistic architecture, known as "Coffee Shop Moderne," which inspired numerous imitators and shifted the emphasis from car service to indoor dining.

The 1950s saw the hamburger increase so much in popularity that it became symbolic of America around the world. To speed things up and save on personnel, drive-ins introduced electronic ordering devices. And to compete with the drive-in, the introduction of the backyard grill inspired burger cookouts that developed into a favorite pastime, and magazines and cookbooks of the decade offered numerous recipes for making burgers at home.

In 1953, the McDonald brothers sold their first franchise in Phoenix, Arizona, and introduced a modern red-and-white building sporting gigantic golden arches. Its immediate success spawned countless imitators, one of the first being Burger King, which opened in Miami.

In 1954, the McDonalds granted exclusive U.S. franchise rights to Ray Kroc, who opened his first McDonald's franchise in Des Plaines, Illinois. Kroc bought out the McDonald brothers in 1961 for $2.7 million. From that point on, burger sales were measured in the millions, then in billions. By 1965, when McDonald's Corporation went public, its theme song, "You Deserve a Break Today," ranked second only to our national anthem in public recognition.

In 1967, big food corporations got into the burger business: General Foods purchased the Burger Chefs chain, Pillsbury bought Burger King, and Ralston Purina acquired Jack in the Box. Not afraid to compete with the giant corporations, Dave Thomas of Columbus, Ohio, started up Wendy's, named after his daughter, and offered made-to-order burgers, to which Burger King responded with their "have it your way" slogan. The next couple of decades saw burgers get bigger, if not better, with introductions of the Big Mac, the Whopper, and the Jumbo Jack.

By 1982, what had become the big three burger chains—McDonalds, Burger King, and Wendy's—launched all-out burger wars in the media, spending massive amounts in advertising and challenging their competition's quality. The Wendy's "Where's the Beef?" advertising campaign proved to be one of the most memorable of all time.

Trying to compete with the fast-food burger trend that was sweeping America, restaurant chefs added high-quality burgers to their menus. Restaurant trade journals in 1984 hailed "gourmet burgers" as the year's biggest trend.

In 1990, as a campaign to encourage the sale of wine during the slow summer months, Sutter Home staged the first Build a Better Burger nationwide recipe contest. By 2004, the annual contest had grown to become one of the top five cooking contests in the nation.

America's love affair with burgers shows no sign of diminishing. It has been reported that Americans eat an average of three burgers per week per person, a figure that includes burgers made from all types of protein purchased from fast-food chains to upscale restaurants as well as those made at home.

Buddy Botts Blinger, the national Pace winner, retired U.S. Army colonel Jim Prescott stood out in a more than 45,000 other July twenty-two states. He remains active in cooking competitions. He's a frequent winner on the International Chili Cooking circuit, competed twice as a finalist in the Pillsbury Bake-Off, and has been a guest chef at the James Beard House in New York.

1990

21

Winner

Jim Pleasants
Williamsburg, Virginia

Prize

Grand Prize, 1990

**Chef Starr's
Wine Pairing**

Zinfandel

Recipe Inspiration
The inspiration for
his Italian-influenced
burger came from his
herb garden: "I grow
lots of herbs and I
wanted to incorporate
some of them in
a burger."

Napa Valley Basil-Smoked Burgers

Pesto Mayonnaise

2/3 cup mayonnaise

2 tablespoons prepared basil pesto

Patties

2 pounds ground sirloin

1/4 cup Zinfandel

1/4 cup lightly packed minced fresh basil

1/4 cup minced red onion

1/4 cup fresh Italian bread crumbs

8 sun-dried tomatoes packed in olive oil,
  finely chopped

2 teaspoons garlic salt

Vegetable oil, for brushing on the grill rack

8 large basil sprigs, moistened with water,
  for grilling

6 large seeded sandwich rolls, split

6 slices Monterey Jack cheese

6 red leaf lettuce leaves

6 (1/4-inch-thick) large tomato slices

6 paper-thin red onion slices, separated
  into rings

6 basil sprigs, for serving

• Prepare a medium-hot fire in a charcoal grill with a cover, or preheat a gas grill to medium-high.

• To make the mayonnaise, combine the ingredients in a small bowl and mix well. Cover and refrigerate until needed.

• To make the patties, combine the sirloin, Zinfandel, basil, onion, bread crumbs, sun-dried tomatoes, and garlic salt in a large bowl. Handling the meat as little as possible to avoid compacting it, mix well. Divide the mixture into 6 equal portions and form the portions into patties to fit the rolls.

• When the grill is ready, brush the grill rack with vegetable oil. Toss the moistened basil sprigs directly onto the fire. Place the patties on the rack, cover, and cook, turning once, until done to preference, 5 to 7 minutes on each side for medium. During the last few minutes of cooking, place the rolls, cut side down, on the outer edges of the rack to toast lightly. During the last minute of cooking, top each patty with a cheese slice.

• To assemble the burgers, spread the mayonnaise over the cut sides of the rolls. On each roll bottom, place a lettuce leaf, a patty, a tomato slice, an onion slice, and a basil sprig. Add the roll tops and serve. *Makes 6 burgers*

Mustard-Grilled Lamb Burgers with Grilled Eggplant Salsa

Basil Yogurt

½ cup plain yogurt

2 tablespoons chopped fresh basil

½ cup sour cream

Grilled Eggplant Salsa

1 large eggplant, sliced crosswise ¾ inch thick

½ small yellow onion, unpeeled, halved

Olive oil, for brushing on the vegetables

½ teaspoon chile powder

1 teaspoon salt

1 teaspoon ground cumin

2 tablespoons diced bottled roasted red bell pepper

1 tablespoon balsamic or red wine vinegar

Patties

1¼ pounds ground extra-lean lamb

1¼ cups minced fresh mushrooms (about 5 ounces)

½ cup chopped hazelnuts (about 2½ ounces)

1 garlic clove, minced or pressed

1 egg white, lightly beaten

1 teaspoon salt

¼ teaspoon freshly ground black pepper

Dijon mustard, for spreading on the patties

8 hamburger buns, split

8 lettuce leaves

- To make the basil yogurt, combine the yogurt and basil in a food processor and blend well. Transfer to a small bowl and fold in the sour cream. Cover and refrigerate until serving.

- Prepare a medium-hot fire in a charcoal grill with a cover, or preheat a gas grill to medium-high.

- To make the salsa, brush both sides of each eggplant slice and the cut sides of the onion with olive oil. In a small bowl, stir together the chile powder, salt, and cumin. Sprinkle the spice mixture on both sides of each eggplant slice.

- When the grill is ready, brush the grill rack with vegetable oil. Place the eggplant slices and onion halves on the grill and cover. Cook the eggplant, turning once, until very brown on both sides, 5 to 7 minutes on each side. Cook the onion until the skin is crisp and blackened, about 10 minutes. Transfer the eggplant and onion to a plate to cool. Slip off and discard the skins from the eggplant and onion, then chop coarsely. In a bowl, lightly combine the eggplant, onion, red pepper, and vinegar; set aside.

- To make the patties, combine the lamb, mushrooms, hazelnuts, garlic, egg white, salt, and pepper in a large bowl. Handling the meat as little as possible to avoid compacting it, mix well. Divide the meat mixture into 8 equal portions and form the portions into patties to fit the buns.

- Brush the grill rack with vegetable oil. Place the patties on the rack, cover, and cook until browned on the bottom, about 4 minutes. With a wide spatula, turn the patties, generously spread the tops of the patties with mustard, and cook until done to preference, about 4 minutes longer for medium-rare. During the last few minutes of cooking, place the buns, cut side down, on the outer edges of the rack to toast lightly.

- To assemble the burgers, place a patty on each bun bottom. Spoon the basil yogurt and salsa over the patties, dividing equally, and top with the lettuce leaves. Add the bun tops and serve.

Makes 8 burgers

Winner
Betty Shenberger
Beaverton, Oregon

Prize
Second Place, 1990

**Chef Starr's
Wine Pairing**
Merlot

Spicy Sausage Burgers
with Roasted Pepper Relish

Roasted Pepper Relish

1 large red bell pepper

2 fresh Anaheim or poblano (sometimes sold
   as pasilla) chiles

Vegetable oil, for brushing on the grill rack

Olive oil, for brushing on the vegetables

¾ cup Zinfandel

½ cup chopped red onion

1 teaspoon minced fresh thyme, or
   ⅓ teaspoon crumbled dried thyme

2 tablespoons apple cider vinegar

2 tablespoons firmly packed brown sugar

1 tablespoon olive oil

2 teaspoons Dijon mustard

Patties

1 pound ground turkey

8 ounces andouille or other smoked spicy
   sausage, chopped

¼ cup finely chopped red onion

1 tablespoon chopped fresh thyme,
   or 1 teaspoon crumbled dried thyme

4 sourdough French rolls, split

Olive oil, for brushing on the rolls

● Prepare a medium-hot fire in a charcoal grill with a cover, or preheat a gas grill to medium-high.

● To make the relish, cut down the sides of the bell pepper, following the natural contours of the pepper to form 4 large slices in all. Remove and discard the seeds. Cut the chiles in half lengthwise, and remove and discard the seeds.

● When the grill is ready, brush the grill rack with vegetable oil. Brush the pepper slices and chile halves with olive oil and place them on the rack. Cover and cook, turning several times, until tender, 4 to 5 minutes on each side.

● Meanwhile, pour the Zinfandel into a fire-proof saucepan and place on the rack alongside the peppers. Bring to a boil and cook until reduced to 1 tablespoon, about 10 minutes. Remove from the fire and stir in the onion, thyme, vinegar, sugar, 1 tablespoon olive oil, and mustard. When the peppers are tender, peel them and cut into julienne strips; add to the saucepan and mix well. Set aside.

● To make the patties, combine the turkey, sausage, onion, and thyme in a large bowl. Handling the meat as little as possible to avoid compacting it, mix well. Divide the mixture into 4 equal portions and form the portions into patties to fit the rolls.

● Place the patties on the grill rack, cover, and cook, turning once, just until the juices run clear when the patties are pierced in the center, about 4 minutes on each side. During the last few minutes of cooking, place the rolls, cut side down, on the outer edges of the rack to toast lightly.

● To assemble the burgers, brush the cut sides of the rolls with olive oil. On each roll bottom, place a patty and top with an equal portion of the pepper relish. Add the roll tops and serve.

Makes 4 burgers

Hearty Southern Bean Burgers

Patties

2 cups cooked or canned black-eyed peas, drained

1 yellow onion, chopped

1 egg, lightly beaten

¼ teaspoon salt

¼ teaspoon freshly ground black pepper

2 tablespoons ketchup

1 tablespoon Worcestershire sauce

Vegetable oil, for brushing on the patties

All-purpose flour, for dusting the patties

Vegetable oil, for brushing on the grill rack

6 hamburger buns, split

Mustard of choice

Mayonnaise or sandwich spread

Ketchup

18 bread-and-butter or dill pickle slices

6 tomato slices

6 lettuce leaves

● Prepare a medium-hot fire in a charcoal grill with a cover, or preheat a gas grill to medium-high.

● To make the patties, mash the peas in a large bowl with a fork. Add the onion, egg, salt, pepper, ketchup, and Worcestershire sauce; mix well. Divide the mixture into 6 equal portions and form the portions into patties to fit the buns. Lightly brush the patties on both sides with oil, then lightly dust with flour.

● When the grill is ready, brush the grill rack with vegetable oil. Place the patties on the rack, cover, and cook, turning once very carefully, until well browned, firm to the touch, and no longer gooey when cut into with a small, sharp knife, 5 to 6 minutes on each side. During the last few minutes of cooking, place the buns, cut side down, on the outer edges of the rack to toast lightly.

● To assemble the burgers, generously spread the cut sides of the buns with mustard, mayonnaise, and ketchup. On each bun bottom, place a patty, 3 pickle slices, a tomato slice, and a lettuce leaf. Add the bun tops and serve. *Makes 6 burgers*

"The Grand Prize winner's name was read aloud, but nobody moved," reminisces Robert Chirico,

a lifelong artist, who later also worked as creative director for a major food public relations firm and now

writes about food and drink. "Well, let's face it—it wasn't the first time someone mangled my name.

I was handed the oversized check, just like the ones I had so often seen on quiz shows in my youth,

and asked to say a few words. A Frank Loesser song immediately sprang to mind. I said, 'I'm the most

happy fella in the whole Napa Valley.' I don't know if anyone knew what I was referring to, but what

I said could not have described better how I felt at that moment."

1991

Winner

Robert Chirico
Greenfield, Massachusetts

Prize

Grand Prize, 1991

**Chef Starr's
Wine Pairing**

Cabernet Sauvignon

Recipe Inspiration

"I like to mix lamb with
beef for flavor, and generally add what I would call
a moistening agent; my
recipe used feta cheese
and Kalamata olives to
this end. I served it with a
cilantro-mint chutney on
a special, thick pita bread
made by Father Sam's
Bakery of Buffalo, New
York, that I brought with
me to Napa Valley."

Lamburgers à la Grecque with Cilantro-Mint Chutney

Cilantro-Mint Chutney

⅓ cup plain yogurt

2 tablespoons chopped onion

1½ fresh jalapeño chiles, seeded and chopped

1½ tablespoons chopped fresh ginger

⅓ cup fresh mint leaves

¾ cup cilantro leaves

1 large garlic clove, chopped

½ teaspoon kosher salt

Pinch of sugar

Patties

1 pound lean ground lamb

1 pound ground sirloin

1 garlic clove, minced

½ cup crumbled feta cheese

⅓ cup Kalamata olives, minced

1 teaspoon kosher salt

¼ cup extra virgin olive oil

1 teaspoon ground cumin mixed with
   1 teaspoon ground coriander

Olive oil, for brushing on the grill rack

6 thick pita breads

6 tomato slices

6 thin red onion slices

6 red leaf lettuce leaves

● To make the chutney, combine all of the ingredients in a blender or food processor and blend thoroughly. Cover and refrigerate until serving.

● Prepare a medium-hot fire in a charcoal grill with a cover, or preheat a gas grill to medium-high.

● To make the patties, combine the lamb, sirloin, garlic, cheese, olives, and salt in a large bowl. Handling the meat as little as possible to avoid compacting it, mix well. Divide the mixture into 6 equal portions and form the portions into patties to fit the pita breads. Brush the patties with the ¼ cup olive oil, then sprinkle with the spice mixture.

● When the grill is ready, brush the grill rack with olive oil. Place the patties on the rack, cover, and cook, turning once, until done to preference, about 4 minutes on each side for medium-rare. During the last few minutes of grilling, place the pita breads on the outer edges of the rack and toast lightly.

● To assemble the burgers, slice off and discard about one-fourth of each pita bread and carefully spread the bread apart to form a pocket. Stuff a patty into each pocket and spoon an equal portion of the chutney over each patty. Add a tomato slice, an onion slice, and a lettuce leaf in each pocket and serve. *Makes 6 burgers*

Hazelnut-Crusted Lamb Burgers

Patties

2 pounds ground lamb

½ cup Cabernet Sauvignon

½ cup minced red onion

½ cup fresh Italian bread crumbs

2 tablespoons chopped fresh flat-leaf parsley

1 tablespoon chopped fresh basil, or

    1 teaspoon crumbled dried basil

1 tablespoon chopped fresh rosemary, or

    1 teaspoon crumbled dried rosemary

1 tablespoon chopped fresh thyme, or

    1 teaspoon crumbled dried thyme

1 garlic clove, minced

½ teaspoon salt

¼ teaspoon freshly ground black pepper

½ cup chopped blanched hazelnuts

¼ cup unseasoned dried Italian bread crumbs

Vegetable oil, for brushing on the grill rack

6 large sesame seed sandwich buns, split

6 tablespoons fresh goat cheese

    (about 3 ounces)

¼ cup Dijon mustard

1 bunch spinach leaves

6 large tomato slices

● Prepare a medium-hot fire in a charcoal grill with a cover, or preheat a gas grill to medium-high.

● To make the patties, combine the lamb, Cabernet Sauvignon, onion, fresh bread crumbs, parsley, basil, rosemary, thyme, garlic, salt, and pepper in a large bowl. Handling the meat as little as possible to avoid compacting it, mix well. Divide the mixture into 6 equal portions and form the portions into patties to fit the buns. On a plate, combine the hazelnuts and dried bread crumbs. Press both sides of each patty into the nut mixture, coating evenly.

● When the grill is ready, brush the grill rack with vegetable oil. Place the patties on the rack, cover, and cook, turning once, until done to preference, about 4 minutes on each side for medium-rare. During the last few minutes of cooking, place the buns, cut side down, on the outer edges of the rack to toast lightly. During the last minute of cooking, top each patty with 1 tablespoon of the cheese.

● To assemble the burgers, spread the mustard over the cut sides of the buns. On each bun bottom, place several spinach leaves, a patty, and a tomato slice. Add the bun tops and serve. *Makes 6 burgers*

Winner
Debbie Russell
Colorado Springs, Colorado

Prize
First Prize, 1991

**Chef Starr's
Wine Pairing**
Merlot

Winner
Caryl Welsh
Clarksville, Maryland

Prize
Second Prize, 1991

**Chef Starr's
Wine Pairing**
Zinfandel

Italian Burgers with Confetti Salsa

Confetti Salsa

1 large tomato, chopped

1 small mango, green or green and
   part yellow, chopped

6 pitted dried plums (prunes), chopped

¼ cup chopped shallots

¼ cup chopped cilantro

1 garlic clove, minced or pressed

Juice of 1 lime

½ fresh jalapeño chile, diced, or to taste

Patties

1 pound hot Italian sausage

1 pound ground turkey

⅔ cup small pimiento-stuffed green olives,
   chopped

15 pitted dried plums (prunes), chopped

1½ tablespoons chopped fresh basil, or
   ½ teaspoon crumbled dried basil

1½ tablespoons chopped fresh flat-leaf parsley

¼ cup Zinfandel

Vegetable oil, for brushing on the grill rack

6 seeded rolls, split

- To make the salsa, combine all of the ingredients in a bowl and mix well. Cover and set aside to allow the flavors to blend.

- Prepare a medium-hot fire in a charcoal grill with a cover, or preheat a gas grill to medium-high.

- To make the patties, combine the sausage, turkey, olives, dried plums, basil, parsley, and Zinfandel in a large bowl. Handling the meat as little as possible to avoid compacting it, mix well. Divide the mixture into 6 equal portions and form the portions into patties to fit the rolls.

- When the grill is ready, brush the grill rack with vegetable oil. Place the patties on the rack, cover, and cook, turning once, just until the juices run clear when the patties are pierced in the center, about 4 minutes on each side. During the last few minutes of cooking, place the rolls, cut side down, around the outer edges of the rack to toast lightly.

- To assemble the burgers, place a patty on each roll bottom and top with a spoonful of salsa. Add the roll tops and serve. *Makes 6 burgers*

Calypso Burgers

Calypso Sauce

1 tablespoon olive oil

1 onion, finely chopped

2 garlic cloves, minced

1 small (or ½ large) red bell pepper,
   finely chopped

2 fresh jalapeño chiles, minced

2 tablespoons molasses

¼ cup dark rum

1 teaspoon grated lime zest

1 small (or ½ large) tomato, seeded and diced

1 tablespoon angostura bitters

½ teaspoon salt

Patties

1 pound ground turkey

½ pound bulk hot pork sausage

½ teaspoon salt

¼ teaspoon freshly ground black pepper

½ teaspoon ground cloves

¾ teaspoon curry powder

1 tablespoon freshly squeezed lime juice

Vegetable oil, for brushing on the grill rack

6 seeded sandwich rolls, split

● Prepare a medium-hot fire in a charcoal grill with a cover, or preheat a gas grill to medium-high.

● To make the sauce, heat the olive oil in a fire-proof saucepan on the grill. Add the onion, garlic, bell pepper, and chiles and sauté until softened, about 5 minutes. Add the molasses, rum, and lime zest. Cook, stirring, until the liquid is nearly all cooked away, about 5 minutes. Stir in the tomato, bitters, and salt and move the saucepan to the edge of the grill rack to keep warm.

● To make the patties, combine the turkey, sausage, salt, pepper, cloves, curry powder, and lime juice in a large bowl. Handling the meat as little as possible to avoid compacting it, mix well. Divide the mixture into 6 equal portions and form the portions into patties to fit the rolls.

● When the grill is ready, brush the grill rack with vegetable oil. Place the patties on the rack, cover, and cook, turning once, just until the juices run clear when the patties are pierced in the center, about 4 minutes on each side. During the last few minutes of cooking, place the rolls, cut side down, on the outer edges of the rack to toast lightly.

● To assemble the burgers, on each roll bottom, place a patty and top with an equal portion of the sauce. Add the roll tops and serve. *Makes 6 burgers*

Winner

Dr. Helen Conwell

Fairhope, Alabama

Prize

Third Prize, 1991

**Chef Starr's
Wine Pairing**

White Cabernet

Winner

Theodore Skiba

Tequesta, Florida

Prize

Award for Creativity, 1991

**Chef Starr's
Wine Pairing**

Pinot Grigio

Three-Nut Turkey Burgers with Tropical Fruit Salsa

Tropical Fruit Salsa

½ carambola (star fruit), cut into ¼-inch dice

⅓ large ripe mango, cut into ¼-inch dice

½ cup red seedless grapes, coarsely chopped

1 banana, cut into ½-inch dice

⅓ cantaloupe, cut into ¼-inch dice

½ cup diced pineapple, fresh or packed in
    its own juice

1 jalapeño chile, cut into very fine dice

Grated zest and juice of 1 lime

¼ cup freshly squeezed orange juice

Patties

½ cup hazelnuts

½ cup almonds

½ cup walnuts

1 tablespoon peanut oil

2 cups shredded Monterey Jack cheese
    (about 6 ounces)

1 pound ground turkey

Vegetable oil, for brushing on the grill rack

4 whole-wheat hamburger buns, split

4 red leaf lettuce leaves

- To make the salsa, combine all of the ingredients in a bowl and stir to blend well. Cover and refrigerate until serving.

- Prepare a hot fire in a charcoal grill with a cover, or preheat a gas grill to high.

- To make the patties, coarsely chop ⅓ cup of each of the nuts. Heat the peanut oil in a nonstick skillet over medium-high heat. Add the chopped nuts and sauté until lightly toasted. Combine the toasted nuts with 1 cup of the cheese in a small bowl and set aside. Transfer the remaining nuts to a food processor, grind finely, and set aside.

- Divide the turkey into 8 equal portions and form the portions into patties to fit the buns. Place equal amounts of the nut-cheese mixture on the center of 4 of the patties. Cover the filling with the remaining 4 patties and press all around to seal the edges. Spread the reserved ground nuts on a flat plate and firmly press both sides of the patties into the nuts.

- When the grill is ready, brush the grill rack with vegetable oil. Place the patties on the rack, cover, and cook, turning once, just until the juices run clear, about 4 minutes on each side. After flipping the patties, sprinkle equal portions of the remaining cheese on the tops to melt. During the last few minutes of cooking, place the buns, cut side down, on the outer edges of the rack to toast lightly.

- To assemble the burgers, on each bun bottom, place 2 to 3 tablespoons of the salsa, a patty, 1 more tablespoon of the salsa, and a lettuce leaf. Add the bun tops and serve.

Makes 4 burgers

After accepting his Grand Prize, a very surprised seventy-six-year-old Robert Allen confided to an

interviewer, "I'm not a cook. My interest in food and flavors is an outgrowth of my early chemistry training."

After retiring as VP of an iron and steel company, a trip to New Zealand inspired Robert to start a food

import business for his pleasure. An entrepreneur and philanthropist in his later years, Robert's interest

in adding new flavors to traditional foods continued after he moved from Washington to the Big Island of

Hawaii, where he passed away in 1999.

1993

Winner

Robert Allen
Port Townsend, Washington

Grand Prize, 1993

**Chef Starr's
Wine Pairing**

White Zinfandel

Recipe Inspiration

Robert's son Peter
remembers his father
always trying exotic
combinations of food
or new flavors. "Dad
was very excited about
entering the contest.
He bought a grill and
used his family as taste-
testers for his recipes
when preparing for
the cook-off."

Gingered-Beef Burgers

Grilled and Onion

1 jicama

1 large sweet onion

2 teaspoons mirin (Japanese sweet rice wine for cooking)

2 teaspoons soy sauce

Patties

1 pound ground beef

4 teaspoons very finely chopped Australian crystallized ginger

¼ cup White Zinfandel

1 tablespoon soy sauce

2 teaspoons mirin

½ teaspoon onion salt

½ teaspoon garlic salt

½ teaspoon freshly ground black pepper

Vegetable oil, for brushing on the grill rack

4 seeded sandwich rolls, split

½ cup butter, softened

• Prepare a medium-hot fire in a charcoal grill with a cover, or preheat a gas grill to medium-high.

• To make the grilled vegetables, peel and slice the jicama and onion into ⅛-inch-thick slices. Place in a bowl and add the mirin and soy sauce. Rotate around so that all sides of the slices are moistened.

• To make the patties, combine the beef, ginger, White Zinfandel, soy sauce, mirin, onion salt, garlic salt, and pepper in a large bowl. Handling the meat as little as possible to avoid compacting it, mix well. Divide the mixture into 4 equal portions and form the portions into patties to fit the rolls.

• When the grill is ready, brush the grill rack with vegetable oil. Place the patties on the rack, cover, and cook, turning once, until done to preference, 5 to 7 minutes on each side for medium. Grill the jicama and onion slices until lightly browned, about 5 minutes on each side. During the last few minutes of cooking, place the rolls, cut side down, on the outer edges of the rack to toast lightly.

• To assemble the burgers, spread the butter over the cut sides of the rolls. On each roll bottom, place a jicama slice, a patty, and an onion slice. Add the roll tops and serve.

Makes 4 burgers

Peppered Jamaican Jerk Burgers Normandy

Jerk Seasoning

1 tablespoon chili powder

2 teaspoons crumbled dried thyme

1½ teaspoons curry powder

1 teaspoon ground cumin

1 teaspoon paprika

1 teaspoon salt

½ teaspoon granulated garlic

½ teaspoon ground cardamom

½ teaspoon ground allspice

½ teaspoon ground cayenne

Sautéed Apples

2 large apples, peeled, cored, and thinly sliced

3 tablespoons Zinfandel

1 tablespoon butter

¼ cup firmly packed light brown sugar

Patties

1 pound ground pork

1 pound ground chuck or sirloin

½ cup fresh bread crumbs

¼ cup Zinfandel

¼ cup finely chopped red onion

2 tablespoons minced fresh ginger

1½ tablespoons crushed black peppercorns

Vegetable oil, for brushing on the grill rack

6 Kaiser rolls, split

¼ cup Jamaican jerk pepper sauce

● To make the seasoning, combine all of the ingredients in a small bowl, mix well, and set aside.

● Prepare a medium-hot fire in a charcoal grill with a cover, or preheat a gas grill to medium-high.

● To make the sautéed apples, place the apples, Zinfandel, and butter in a fire-proof skillet on the grill rack. Sauté until the apples begin to soften, about 8 minutes. Add the brown sugar and cook until the liquid is reduced and syrupy, about 4 minutes. Set aside.

● To make the patties, combine the jerk seasoning, pork, beef, bread crumbs, Zinfandel, onion, and ginger. Handling the meat as little as possible to avoid compacting it, mix well. Divide the mixture into 6 equal portions and form the portions into patties to fit the rolls. Sprinkle both sides of the patties with the crushed peppercorns.

● When the grill is ready, brush the grill rack with vegetable oil. Place the patties on the rack, cover, and cook, turning once, until done to preference, 5 to 7 minutes on each side for medium. During the last few minutes of cooking, place the rolls, cut side down, on the outer edges of the rack to toast lightly.

● To assemble the burgers, spread the pepper sauce over the cut sides of the rolls. On each roll bottom, place a patty and an equal portion of the sautéed apples. Add the roll tops and serve. *Makes 6 burgers*

Winner

Caryl Welsh

Clarksville, Maryland

Prize

Second Prize, 1993

**Chef Starr's
Wine Pairing**

Chardonnay

Choucroute Burgers with Green Apple Salsa

Green Apple Salsa

1 Granny Smith apple, peeled, cored, and diced

1 garlic clove

¼ cup white wine Worcestershire sauce

Patties

¾ pound ground turkey

¾ pound hot Italian sausage

1¼ cups sauerkraut (from a jar or
   plastic package, not canned), drained
   and firmly packed

4 garlic cloves, minced

2 tablespoons minced shallot

1½ tablespoons caraway seeds

½ teaspoon minced canned chipotle chiles
   in adobo sauce

1 tablespoon adobo sauce from canned chiles

½ teaspoon ground paprika

Olive oil, for brushing on the grill rack and
   the bread

8 crusty rye bread slices

4 ounces Saint-André cheese or
   other triple-cream cheese

• To make the salsa, combine all of the ingredients in a small bowl. Set aside to allow the flavors to blend while preparing the burgers.

• Prepare a medium-hot fire in a charcoal grill with a cover, or preheat a gas grill to medium-high.

• To make the patties, combine the turkey, sausage, sauerkraut, garlic, shallot, caraway seeds, chipotle chile, adobo sauce, and paprika in a large bowl. Handling the meat as little as possible to avoid compacting it, mix well. Divide the mixture into 4 equal portions and form the portions into patties to fit the bread slices.

• When the grill is ready, brush the grill rack with olive oil. Place the patties on the rack, cover, and cook, turning once, just until the juices run clear when the patties are pierced in the center, about 4 minutes on each side. During the last few minutes of cooking, brush the bread slices on both sides with olive oil and place on the outer edges of the rack, turning once, to toast lightly.

• To assemble the burgers, spread one side of each bread slice with an equal portion of the cheese. On 4 of the bread slices, cheese side up, place a patty and a spoonful of the salsa. Add the remaining bread slices, cheese side down, and serve. *Makes 4 burgers*

Tuscan Burgers Bruschetta

Tomato Topping

1 ripe tomato, chopped

2 garlic cloves, minced

2 tablespoons minced fresh flat-leaf parsley

3 tablespoons minced fresh basil

3 tablespoons extra virgin olive oil

3 tablespoons freshly grated Parmesan cheese

Salt

Freshly ground black pepper

Patties

1 scant cup loosely packed crumbled
    Gorgonzola cheese

2 tablespoons finely minced fresh flat-leaf
    parsley

3 tablespoons chopped onion

2 pounds ground round

Salt

Freshly ground black pepper

Vegetable oil, for brushing on the grill rack

4 thin prosciutto or unsmoked ham slices

½ pound coarsely grated Fontina cheese

Bruschetta

1 oblong loaf crusty Italian bread, sliced
    diagonally into 12 (½- to ¾-inch-thick) slices

Extra virgin olive oil, for brushing on the bread

• Prepare a medium-hot fire in a charcoal grill with a cover, or preheat a gas grill to medium-high.

• To make the topping, combine all of the ingredients, including salt and pepper to taste, in a bowl and mix well. Set aside.

• To make the patties, combine the Gorgonzola, parsley, and onion in a large bowl. Add the beef and season with salt and pepper. Handling the meat as little as possible to avoid compacting it, mix well. Divide the mixture into 6 equal portions and form the portions into patties to fit the bread slices.

• When the grill is ready, brush the grill rack with vegetable oil. Place the patties on the rack, cover, and cook 5 minutes. Turn the patties and cook 4 minutes. Place a slice of prosciutto on each patty and top with the Fontina, dividing equally. Cover the grill and continue cooking the patties until done to preference, 1 to 4 minutes longer for medium.

• To make the bruschetta, while the patties are cooking, brush the bread slices on each side with olive oil. Place on the outer edges of the grill rack, turning once, to toast lightly.

• To assemble the burgers, spoon half of the tomato topping on 6 of the bruschetta slices, then top with the patties, the remaining tomato topping, and the remaining bruschetta.

Makes 6 burgers

Winner

Janet Steck

Cortland, New York

Prize

Third Prize, 1993

Chef Starr's

Wine Pairing

Shiraz (Syrah)

Winner
Robert Anzovino
San Jose, California

Prize
Award for Creativity, 1993

**Chef Starr's
Wine Pairing**
Gewürztraminer

Beijing Burgers

Five-Spice Grilled Onions

2 yellow onions

Salt

Freshly ground black pepper

2 teaspoons Chinese five-spice powder

4 tablespoons butter

Marinated Daikon

12 ounces daikon, peeled and julienned

1 teaspoon salt

1 cup rice vinegar

½ cup water

Dried Apricot–Ginger Sauce

20 dried apricot halves

4 teaspoons minced fresh ginger

Water to cover

Salt

Freshly ground black pepper

Patties

1 pound raw shrimp

12 large dried black Chinese mushrooms,
    soaked in warm water until soft

1 pound ground pork

½ cup White Zinfandel

1 tablespoon minced fresh ginger

1 teaspoon salt

2 tablespoons low-sodium soy sauce

2 tablespoons chicken stock or canned broth

¼ cup almond oil

2 tablespoons Asian sesame oil

Vegetable oil, for brushing on the grill rack

6 Vietnamese or sweet French rolls, split

● Prepare a medium-hot fire in a charcoal grill with a cover, or preheat a gas grill to medium-high.

● To make the grilled onions, peel the onions and cut off the tops. Slit each onion down from the top but not completely through the bottom, making 6 attached sections. Sprinkle to taste with salt and pepper and add even amounts of the five-spice powder and butter to the onions where sectioned. Double-wrap each onion in aluminum foil and place directly on the grill fire. Cook until the onions are soft, about 35 minutes.

● To make the marinated daikon, place the daikon in a bowl and add the salt, vinegar, and water. Stir well and set aside.

● To make the sauce, combine all of the ingredients, including salt and pepper to taste, in a small fire-proof saucepan, set on the grill, and simmer until the apricots are soft, about 15 minutes. Transfer to a food processor and purée until a thick paste is formed, adding some of the vinegar and water mixture from the daikon as needed to thin the consistency. Set aside.

● To make the patties, shell and devein the shrimp. Wash, drain, and pat dry with paper towels. Chop medium fine and set aside. Discard the mushroom stems and cut the caps into ½-inch shreds and set aside. Place the pork in a bowl and add the White Zinfandel while stirring until the meat holds together. Add the shrimp, mushrooms, ginger, salt, soy sauce,

(continued)

chicken stock, almond oil, and sesame oil. Handling the meat as little as possible to avoid compacting it, mix well. Divide the mixture into 6 equal portions and form the portions into patties to fit the rolls.

● When the grill is ready, brush the grill rack with vegetable oil. Place the patties on the rack, cover, and cook, turning once, until done to preference, 4 to 5 minutes on each side for medium. During the last few minutes of cooking, place the rolls, cut side down, on the outer edges of the rack to toast lightly.

● To assemble the burgers, drain the daikon well. On each roll bottom, place a patty, two sections of the grilled onions, an equal portion of the marinated daikon, and an equal portion of the sauce. Add the roll tops and serve. *Makes 6 burgers*

A sales compensation manager for a large telecommunications firm in

California's Silicon Valley, Kurt Wait found his prize-winning burger creativity

in the contest's setting—Napa Valley. During the cook-off weekend, the valley continued to inspire Kurt.

"My sister and I stayed in a little cottage inside a vineyard not far from town. A tranquil setting with some

nice wine and fruit. I couldn't have asked for more. The thing I remember the most, however, was the relief

I felt when I finished putting together my last burger just as the judges walked up to my station. For the

last half hour or so, I was certain that I would not finish in time. I've never worked so feverishly."

Two years after his BBB win, Kurt became the first person to win the $1,000,000 Grand Prize in the

Pillsbury Bake-Off® and remains the only man ever to win that venerable contest.

1994

Winner

Kurt Wait
Redwood City, California

Prize

Grand Prize, 1994

**Chef Starr's
Wine Pairing**

Pinot Noir

Recipe Inspiration
"Napa Valley was
the inspiration for
my portobello burger.
Local wine and
cheese, fresh herbs and
greens, beautiful
scenery and weather—
what could be more
inspirational?"

Portobello Burgers

Sun-Dried Tomato Mayonnaise

⅓ cup mayonnaise

¼ cup chopped sun-dried tomatoes packed
   in olive oil, drained

Spice Mixture

2 tablespoons chopped fresh thyme

1 tablespoon chopped fresh oregano

1 teaspoon salt

1 teaspoon freshly ground black pepper

Grilled Portobellos

¼ cup Zinfandel

2 tablespoons olive oil

1 teaspoon grated lemon zest

4 portobello mushrooms, stems removed

Patties

1½ pounds ground chuck

3 tablespoons Zinfandel

2 shallots, finely chopped

2 teaspoons ground cumin

¼ teaspoon ground cayenne

Vegetable oil, for brushing on the grill rack

4 round focaccia rolls or onion rolls, split

16 arugula leaves

½ cup fresh goat cheese (about 4 ounces)

- Prepare a medium-hot fire in a charcoal grill with a cover, or preheat a gas grill to medium-high.

- To make the mayonnaise, combine the mayonnaise and the sun-dried tomatoes in a small bowl and mix well. Cover and refrigerate until serving.

- To make the spice mixture, combine all of the ingredients in a small bowl and mix well. Set aside.

- To make the grilled portobellos, combine the Zinfandel, olive oil, lemon zest, and 1 tablespoon of the spice mixture in a shallow container and whisk to blend well. Add the mushrooms and turn to coat with the marinade. Set aside.

- To make the patties, combine the beef, Zinfandel, shallots, cumin, cayenne, and remaining spice mixture in a large bowl. Handling the meat as little as possible to avoid compacting it, mix well. Divide the mixture into 4 equal portions and form the portions into patties to fit the rolls.

- Drain the mushrooms, reserving the marinade.

- When the grill is ready, brush the grill rack with vegetable oil. Place the patties and the mushrooms on the rack, cover, and cook, turning once, until the patties are done to preference, 5 to 7 minutes on each side for medium, and the mushrooms are tender, 5 to 10 minutes. Brush the mushrooms frequently with the reserved marinade. During the last few minutes of cooking, place the rolls, cut side down, on the outer edges of the rack to toast lightly.

- To assemble the burgers, spread the mayonnaise over the cut sides of the rolls. On each roll bottom, place 4 arugula leaves, a patty, 2 tablespoons of the goat cheese, and a mushroom. Add the roll tops and serve. *Makes 4 burgers*

Peppered Lamb Burgers with "Hot Tomato" Jam

"Hot Tomato" Jam

4 cups ripe tomatoes, peeled, cored, and
    roughly chopped (for best results, use a
    variety of tomatoes)

⅓ cup sugar

3 tablespoons finely minced fresh ginger

2 tablespoons unseasoned rice vinegar

1 teaspoon hot pepper sauce

3 tablespoons fresh basil, cut into chiffonade

Salt

Patties

1⅓ pounds freshly ground lamb

2 tablespoons five-peppercorn blend,
    cracked or very coarsely ground

1 garlic clove, finely minced

2 tablespoons sesame oil

¼ cup Merlot

Salt

Olive oil, for brushing on the grill rack

4 hamburger buns, split

4 red leaf lettuce leaves

● Prepare a medium-hot fire in a charcoal grill with a cover, or preheat a gas grill to medium-high.

● To make the jam, combine the tomatoes, sugar, ginger, vinegar, and ½ teaspoon of the pepper sauce in a flame-proof nonreactive saucepan. Place the pan on the grill rack and bring the mixture to a slow simmer. Continue simmering, stirring occasionally and moving on and off the heat as necessary, until the mixture is reduced by half, about 30 minutes. Move the pan to the coolest part of the rack and continue to cook for another 15 minutes. Taste and add the remaining pepper sauce to taste. Continue cooking until the mixture reaches a jam-like consistency, and then remove from the heat and set aside to cool. Stir the basil into the cooled mixture and season to taste with salt. Set aside.

● To make the patties, combine the lamb, peppercorn blend, garlic, sesame oil, and Merlot in a large bowl and season with salt. Handling the meat as little as possible to avoid compacting it, mix well. Divide the mixture into 4 equal portions and form the portions into patties to fit the buns.

● Brush the grill rack with olive oil. Place the patties on the rack, cover, and cook, turning once, until done to preference, about 4 minutes on each side for medium-rare. During the last few minutes of cooking, place the buns, cut side down, on the outer edges of the rack to toast lightly.

● To assemble the burgers, spread the cut sides of the buns with the tomato jam. On each bun bottom, place a lettuce leaf and a patty. Add the bun tops and serve. *Makes 4 burgers*

Winner
Nancy Strande
Snohomish, Washington

Prize
First Prize, 1994

**Chef Starr's
Wine Pairing**
Merlot

Winner

Ellen Burr

Truro, Massachusetts

Prize

Second Prize, 1994

**Chef Starr's
Wine Pairing**

Merlot

Brazilian Burgers

Marinade

1 tablespoon pressed garlic

1½ teaspoons coarse salt

⅓ cup red wine vinegar

¼ teaspoon crushed red pepper flakes

1 teaspoon dried oregano

1 teaspoon ground cumin

¼ teaspoon ground allspice

Patties

1 pound ground pork

¼ cup yellow cornmeal

Black Bean Spread

1 (15- to 16-ounce) can black beans, rinsed
   and drained

1 tablespoon olive oil

2 tablespoons chopped cilantro

1 Spanish onion, thinly sliced

1 red bell pepper, seeded and quartered

1 green bell pepper, seeded and quartered

Vegetable oil, for brushing on the peppers
   and the grill rack

4 Kaiser rolls, split

2 blood oranges, peeled, ends trimmed,
   and each cut into 4 rounds

2 tablespoons chopped cilantro

- Prepare a medium-hot fire in a charcoal grill with a cover, or preheat a gas grill to medium-high.

- To make the marinade, combine all of the ingredients in a small bowl and mix well.

- To make the patties, combine the pork and cornmeal with half of the marinade in a large bowl. Handling the meat as little as possible to avoid compacting it, mix well. Divide the mixture into 4 equal portions and form the portions into patties to fit the rolls.

- To make the spread, combine the beans, olive oil, cilantro, and 2 tablespoons of the remaining marinade in a small bowl and coarsely mash the beans with a fork. Set aside.

- Combine the onion and the remaining marinade in a small bowl. Brush the pepper quarters with vegetable oil.

- When the grill is ready, brush the grill rack with vegetable oil. Place the patties on the rack, cover, and cook, turning once, until done to preference, 4 to 5 minutes on each side for medium. Grill the peppers, turning several times, until soft and browned, 4 to 5 minutes on each side. During the last few minutes of cooking, place the rolls, cut side down, on the outer edges of the rack to toast lightly.

- To assemble the burgers, cover the cut sides of the roll bottoms with the bean spread. On each roll bottom, place a patty, a red and green pepper quarter, an orange slice, an equal portion of the marinated onions, and 1½ teaspoons of the cilantro. Add the roll tops and serve. *Makes 4 burgers*

Tropical Burgers

Mango Salsa

2 ripe mangos, peeled, pitted, diced, and
    drained (reserve juice for spread)

1 tablespoon chopped cilantro

1 green onion, finely chopped

1 small fresh jalapeño chile, seeded and
    minced

2 large garlic cloves, minced

Tropical Spread

½ cup cream cheese, softened

2 teaspoons mango juice

2 teaspoons freshly squeezed orange juice

2 tablespoons shredded coconut

Patties

¾ pound ground beef

½ pound ground pork

¼ cup Zinfandel

1 tablespoon soy sauce

1 tablespoon freshly squeezed orange juice

2 teaspoons ground ginger

½ teaspoon garlic salt

Vegetable oil, for brushing on the grill rack

4 seeded hamburger buns, split

2 green onions, finely chopped

● Prepare a medium-hot fire in a charcoal grill with a cover, or preheat a gas grill to medium-high.

● To make the salsa, combine all of the ingredients in a bowl and mix well. Cover and refrigerate until ready to serve. Drain if necessary before using.

● To make the spread, combine the cream cheese, mango juice, and orange juice in a bowl and stir until smooth. Stir in the shredded coconut. Cover and refrigerate until ready to serve.

● To make the patties, combine the beef, pork, Zinfandel, soy sauce, orange juice, ginger, and garlic salt in a large bowl. Handling the meat as little as possible to avoid compacting it, mix well. Divide the mixture into 4 equal portions and form the portions into patties to fit the buns.

● When the grill is ready, brush the grill rack with vegetable oil. Place the patties on the rack, cover, and cook, turning once, until done to preference, 5 to 7 minutes on each side for medium. During the last few minutes of cooking, place the buns, cut side down, on the outer edges of the rack to toast lightly.

● To assemble the burgers, cover the cut sides of the buns with the tropical spread. On each bun bottom, place a patty, an equal portion of the salsa, and an equal portion of the green onion. Add the bun tops and serve. *Makes 4 burgers*

Porter Lansing's win made him the fifth man in a row to win BBB. He credits the cook-off as a life-

changing experience. "The contest and especially the esteemed caliber of the judges gave me, a student

at that time of contemporary American cuisine, the incredible confidence to sell my appliance business

and dive headfirst into the professional cooking world, leading to and culminating in four years cooking

at the top New American Grille in Colorado. I've since lost a leg to an illness and have retired to a budding

career as a food-themed novel author. The experience of the Build a Better Burger contest was primary

in my ability to compose recipes in the regional American genre."

1995

Winner

Porter Lansing
Englewood, Colorado

Prize

Grand Prize, 1995

**Chef Starr's
Wine Pairing**

White Zinfandel

Recipe Inspiration

"I tried to incorporate
sweet, sour, salty,
fragrant, bitter, nutty,
and hot flavors
to create a Chinese
theme for the
ground chicken."

Chicken Oriental Burgers with Grilled Shiitake

Black Bean–Mustard Basting Sauce

½ cup Asian black bean sauce

¼ cup White Zinfandel

2 tablespoons stone ground mustard

2 teaspoons tamari

1 teaspoon prepared horseradish

1 teaspoon onion powder

½ teaspoon garlic powder

¼ teaspoon ground cayenne

Patties

2 tablespoons sesame seeds

2 pounds ground chicken

2 tablespoons hoisin sauce

1 tablespoon chopped cilantro

1 tablespoon finely chopped green onion

1 teaspoon ginger juice

1 teaspoon tamari

1 teaspoon cornstarch

½ teaspoon garlic powder

¼ teaspoon sesame oil

¼ teaspoon hot chile oil

¼ teaspoon freshly ground black pepper

Vegetable oil, for brushing on the grill rack

6 shiitake mushrooms, stems discarded

1 tablespoon Asian sesame oil

6 onion rolls, split

Melted butter, for brushing on the rolls

● To make the basting sauce, combine all of the ingredients in a small fire-proof saucepan and mix well. Set aside.

● Prepare a medium-hot fire in a charcoal grill with a cover, or preheat a gas grill to medium-high.

● To make the patties, toast the sesame seeds in a dry pan on the grill. Let cool and then combine with the chicken, hoisin sauce, cilantro, green onion, ginger juice, tamari, cornstarch, garlic powder, sesame oil, chile oil, and pepper in a large bowl. Handling the meat as little as possible to avoid compacting it, mix well. Divide the mixture into 6 equal portions and form the portions into patties to fit the rolls.

● When the grill is ready, brush the grill rack with vegetable oil. Place the patties on the rack, cover, and cook, turning once and basting frequently with the sauce, just until the juices run clear when the patties are pierced in the center, about 4 minutes on each side. Brush the mushrooms with the sesame oil and grill alongside the patties, turning frequently and brushing with the sauce, until tender, about 10 minutes. During the last few minutes of cooking, brush the cut side of the rolls with melted butter and place, cut side down, on the outer edges of the rack to toast lightly. Place the saucepan on the grill and bring the remaining basting sauce to a boil.

● To assemble the burgers, cut each mushroom into 4 wedges. Brush the basting sauce on the cut sides of the rolls. On each roll bottom, place a patty and 4 mushroom wedges. Add the roll tops and serve. *Makes 6 burgers*

Mediterranean Tuna Burgers with Lemon-Basil Mayonnaise

Lemon-Basil Mayonnaise

½ cup lowfat mayonnaise

1 teaspoon finely grated lemon zest

6 large fresh basil leaves, finely chopped

2 teaspoons brine-packed capers, rinsed and
    drained

Patties

1 pound fresh tuna steaks, trimmed and
    ground

¼ large red bell pepper, finely chopped

1 whole green onion, finely chopped

2 tablespoons Chardonnay

1 tablespoon horseradish mustard

1 tablespoon plus 1 teaspoon olive oil

½ teaspoon seasoned salt

⅓ to ½ cup unseasoned dried Italian
    bread crumbs

Vegetable oil, for brushing on the grill rack

4 seeded hamburger buns, split

4 slices mozzarella or provolone cheese

2 (6-ounce) jars marinated artichoke hearts,
    drained well on paper towels and cut into
    small pieces

Mixed baby greens

● To make the mayonnaise, combine all of the ingredients in a small bowl and mix well. Cover and refrigerate for at least 1 hour before using to allow the flavors to blend.

● Prepare a medium-hot fire in a charcoal grill with a cover, or preheat a gas grill to medium-high.

● To make the patties, combine the tuna, bell pepper, onion, Chardonnay, mustard, olive oil, and seasoned salt in a bowl. Handling the tuna as little as possible to avoid compacting it, mix well, adding just enough bread crumbs to hold the mixture together. Divide the mixture into 4 equal portions and form the portions into patties to fit the buns.

● When the grill is ready, brush the grill rack with vegetable oil. Place the patties on the rack, cover, and cook, turning once, until done to preference, 3 to 4 minutes on each side for medium-rare. During the last few minutes of cooking, place the buns, cut side down, on the outer edges of the rack to toast lightly. During the last minute of cooking, place 1 slice of the cheese on each patty to melt.

● To assemble the burgers, spread the mayonnaise over the cut sides of the buns. On each bun bottom, place an equal portion of the artichoke hearts, a few greens, and a patty. Add the bun tops and serve. *Makes 4 burgers*

Winner

Vincent Grosse

Marietta, Georgia

Prize

First Prize, 1995

Chef Starr's

Wine Pairing

Chardonnay

Winner

Martin Kokotaylo
Sylvania, Ohio

Prize

Second Prize, 1995

**Chef Starr's
Wine Pairing**

Chenin Blanc

Green Chile Chicken Burgers with Orange-Chili Mayonnaise and Three-Pepper Cheese Spread

Orange-Chili Mayonnaise

½ cup mayonnaise

2 tablespoons chopped cilantro

1 tablespoon chopped red onion

2 teaspoons grated orange zest

2 teaspoons chili powder

¼ teaspoon ground cumin

Three-Pepper Cheese Spread

6 ounces fresh goat cheese

1 tablespoon finely minced red bell pepper

1 tablespoon finely minced yellow bell pepper

1 fresh jalapeño chile, seeded and finely minced

Patties

1½ pounds ground chicken

2 garlic cloves, minced

3 fresh green Anaheim chiles, roasted over
    the grill fire, peeled, seeded, and chopped

3 tablespoons Merlot

½ teaspoon ground cinnamon

¼ teaspoon ground cayenne

Vegetable oil, for brushing on the grill rack

4 hamburger buns, split

1 bunch watercress

• Prepare a medium-hot fire in a charcoal grill with a cover, or preheat a gas grill to medium-high.

• To make the mayonnaise, combine all of the ingredients in a small bowl and mix well. Cover and refrigerate until ready to serve.

• To make the spread, mash the cheese with a fork in a small bowl and then stir in the peppers and chile. Cover and refrigerate until ready to serve.

• To make the patties, combine the chicken, garlic, roasted chiles, Merlot, cinnamon, and cayenne in a large bowl. Handling the meat as little as possible to avoid compacting it, mix well. Divide the mixture into 4 equal portions and form the portions into patties to fit the buns.

• When the grill is ready, brush the grill rack with vegetable oil. Place the patties on the rack, cover, and cook, turning once, just until the juices run clear when the patties are pierced in the center, about 4 minutes on each side. During the last few minutes of cooking, place the buns, cut side down, on the outer edges of the rack to toast lightly.

• To assemble the burgers, spread the bun bottoms with the cheese spread and top with an equal portion of the watercress, a patty, and an equal portion of the mayonnaise. Add the bun tops and serve. *Makes 4 burgers*

San Francisco Cioppino Burgers

Golden Gate Mayonnaise

½ cup mayonnaise

¼ cup bottled chili sauce

1½ teaspoons prepared horseradish

Patties

2 leeks, white portion only

4 shallots

½ red bell pepper, cut into large pieces

¼ red onion, cut into large pieces

4 large garlic cloves

⅓ cup Chardonnay

⅓ cup olive oil

Juice of 1 lemon

1 tablespoon dried Italian seasoning herb blend

1½ teaspoons freshly ground black pepper

½ teaspoon crushed red pepper flakes

½ pound bay scallops, cut into halves

½ pound bay shrimp

6 tablespoons double-concentrate tomato paste

¼ cup mayonnaise

1 tablespoon Old Bay seasoning

1 tablespoon minced garlic

1 teaspoon crumbled dried oregano

1 teaspoon grated lemon zest

1 teaspoon salt

4 dashes TABASCO Pepper Sauce, or to taste

⅓ pound skinless red snapper, ground in food processor

Meat from a 1-pound fresh crab, cleaned and shredded

About 2½ cups fresh sourdough bread crumbs

¼ cup butter, softened

1 teaspoon crushed garlic

12 slices sourdough bread (Fisherman's Wharf style)

● To make the mayonnaise, combine all of the ingredients in a bowl and mix well. Cover and refrigerate until serving.

● To make the patties, combine the leeks, shallots, bell pepper, onion, and garlic in a shallow dish. Combine the Chardonnay, olive oil, lemon juice, Italian seasoning, 1 teaspoon of the black pepper, and the red pepper flakes in a small bowl, whisk to blend well, and pour over the vegetables. Set side to marinate for 30 minutes.

● Prepare a medium-hot fire in a charcoal grill with a cover, or preheat a gas grill to medium-high.

● Place the scallops and shrimp in colander set in a sink and drain thoroughly.

● Combine the tomato paste, mayonnaise, Old Bay seasoning, minced garlic, oregano, lemon zest, salt, pepper sauce, and the remaining ½ teaspoon black pepper in a small bowl and stir to mix well. Set aside.

● When the grill is ready, brush the grill rack with some of the vegetable marinade. Place the vegetables on the rack, reserving the marinade, and cook, turning often, until tender, 7 to 10 minutes. Remove the vegetables from the grill, let cool for about 10 minutes, then chop and transfer to a large bowl.

(continued)

Winner
Nicol Spedus
Petaluma, California

Prize
Award for Creativity, 1995

**Chef Starr's
Wine Pairing**
Chardonnay

San Francisco Cioppino Burgers (continued)

- Increase the grill heat to very hot.

- Squeeze and discard the excess liquid from the scallops, shrimp, snapper, and crab and add to the chopped vegetables. Stir in the tomato paste mixture and just enough bread crumbs to hold the mixture together. Handling the seafood as little as possible to avoid compacting it, mix well. Divide the mixture into 6 equal portions and form the portions into patties to fit the bread slices.

- When the grill is ready, brush the grill rack with the reserved marinade. Place the patties on the rack, cover, and cook, turning once, just until opaque throughout, about 4 minutes on each side. Meanwhile, combine the butter and garlic in a small bowl and mix well. Spread the butter mixture on one side of each bread slice. During the last few minutes of cooking the patties, place the bread slices, buttered side down, on the outer edges of the rack, turning once, to toast lightly.

- To assemble the burgers, spread the mayonnaise on the buttered sides of the bread slices. Top 6 slices of bread with patties. Add the remaining bread slices, cut each burger in half, and serve.

Makes 6 burgers

Lori Welander trounced the male-dominated world of backyard

grilling to become the first woman to win BBB. At the time, she was an at-home mom who

had recently sold her fiber-optic company. "The breathtaking setting—anything cooked on those grounds

would be a prizewinner—with the picturesque Victorian Inn in the background, the gardens, and sipping

a glass of wine—it doesn't get much better than that!" recalls Lori of her trip to BBB. Lori has continued

her winning streak with Grand Prizes in the National Beef Cook-Off®, Emeril's ABC Good Morning America

Kicked-Up Recipe Contest, the Southern Living Cook-Off, and several other competitions. She's been

a finalist in the Pillsbury Bake-Off® and twice made the finals of the National Chicken Cooking Contest.

1996

Winner

Lori Welander
Shelburne, Vermont

Prize

Grand Prize, 1996

**Chef Starr's
Wine Pairing**

Sauvignon Blanc

Recipe Inspiration

"Mulligatawny soup,
which I often enjoyed
while working in
England, inspired
my burger."

Mulligatawny Burgers

Curried Apple Mayonnaise

½ cup mayonnaise

3 tablespoons peeled and finely chopped
   tart apple

1 teaspoon Dijon mustard

½ teaspoon curry powder

Pinch of ground cayenne

Patties

½ cup sliced almonds

1½ pounds freshly ground chicken

1 egg white, lightly beaten

2 tablespoons minced green onion

½ cup peeled and finely chopped tart apple

Salt

Freshly ground black pepper

⅓ cup fine fresh bread crumbs

1 teaspoon curry powder

Vegetable oil, for brushing on the grill rack

6 sourdough rolls, split

Young tender spinach leaves

● To make the mayonnaise, combine all of the ingredients in a small bowl and stir to blend well. Cover and refrigerate until serving.

● Prepare a medium-hot fire in a charcoal grill with a cover, or preheat a gas grill to medium-high.

● To make the patties, place the almonds in a small fire-proof skillet on the grill. Stir frequently until lightly golden brown, 5 to 10 minutes, and set aside to cool.

● Combine the chicken, egg white, green onion, and apple in a large bowl and season with salt and pepper. Handling the meat as little as possible to avoid compacting it, mix well. Divide the mixture into 6 equal portions and form the portions into patties to fit the rolls. Finely chop the toasted almonds and combine with the bread crumbs and curry powder in a shallow bowl, stirring well. Coat both sides of the patties with the almond mixture, pressing gently to adhere.

● Brush the grill rack with vegetable oil. Place the patties on the rack, cover, and cook, turning once, just until the juices run clear when the patties are pierced in the center, about 4 minutes on each side. During the last few minutes of cooking, place the rolls, cut side down, on the outer edges of the rack to toast lightly.

● To assemble the burgers, decoratively fan several spinach leaves on the bottom half of each roll and top each with a patty and a generous dollop of the mayonnaise. Add the roll tops and serve. *Makes 6 burgers*

Fresh Salmon Burgers
with Lemon-Cilantro Mayonnaise

Lemon-Cilantro Mayonnaise

⅓ cup mayonnaise

1 cup lightly packed cilantro leaves

¼ teaspoon minced garlic

2 teaspoons freshly squeezed lemon juice

¼ teaspoon freshly ground black pepper

Patties

1½ pounds boneless, skinless salmon fillet

⅓ cup fresh bread crumbs

2 anchovy fillets mashed with 2 tablespoons
    water

1 tablespoon minced shallot

1 tablespoon freshly squeezed lemon juice

1 tablespoon Dijon mustard

½ teaspoon freshly ground black pepper

1 small red onion, sliced

1½ tablespoons unseasoned rice vinegar

Vegetable oil, for brushing on the grill rack

4 sesame seed buns, split

8 fresh spinach leaves

● To make the mayonnaise, combine all of the ingredients in a small bowl and whisk to blend well. Cover and refrigerate until serving.

● To make the patties, with a large chef's knife, cut the salmon into strips. Cut the strips crosswise, then chop until the salmon is the texture of raw hamburger meat. Transfer the salmon to a large bowl and add the bread crumbs, anchovy-water mixture, shallot, lemon juice, mustard, and pepper. Handling the salmon as little as possible to avoid compacting it, mix well. Divide the mixture into 4 equal portions and form the portions into patties to fit the buns. Cover and refrigerate for about 30 minutes.

● Meanwhile, combine the onion and vinegar in a bowl and toss well. Set aside for about 30 minutes, stirring often.

● Prepare a medium-hot fire in a charcoal grill with a cover, or preheat a gas grill to medium-high.

● When the grill is ready, brush the grill rack with vegetable oil. Place the chilled patties on the rack, cover, and cook, turning once, until just opaque throughout, about 2 minutes on each side. During the last few minutes of cooking, place the buns, cut side down, on the outer edges of the rack to toast lightly.

● To assemble the burgers, spread the mayonnaise over the cut sides of the buns. On each bun bottom, place a few spinach leaves, a patty, and an equal portion of the onions. Add the bun tops and serve. *Makes 4 burgers*

Casablanca Burgers with Citrus-Olive Relish and Harissa Aioli

Citrus-Olive Relish

1 small lemon, peeled, seeded, and chopped

1 orange, peeled, seeded, and chopped

1/2 cup chopped red onion

1/3 cup chopped pitted black olives

3 tablespoons chopped cilantro

1 tablespoon chopped fresh mint

1 tablespoon olive oil

Kosher salt

Freshly ground black pepper

Harissa Aioli

1/3 cup mayonnaise

1/4 cup finely chopped roasted red bell pepper

1 teaspoon minced garlic

1 teaspoon freshly squeezed lemon juice

Pinch of ground cayenne

Patties

1 pound ground chuck

1/2 pound ground lamb

1/4 cup Zinfandel

2 shallots, finely chopped

2 tablespoons chopped cilantro

2 tablespoons chopped fresh flat-leaf parsley

1 tablespoon chopped fresh mint

1 1/2 teaspoons ground cumin, toasted

1 teaspoon minced fresh ginger

1/2 teaspoon ground paprika, preferably Hungarian sweet

1/4 teaspoon ground cinnamon

Kosher salt

Freshly ground black pepper

Olive oil, for brushing on the grill rack

4 onion rolls, split

4 red leaf lettuce leaves

● Prepare a medium-hot fire in a charcoal grill with a cover, or preheat a gas grill to medium-high.

● To make the relish, combine all of the ingredients, including salt and pepper to taste, in a bowl and toss to blend well. Set aside.

● To make the aioli, combine all of the ingredients in a bowl and mix well. Cover and refrigerate until serving.

● To make the patties, combine the beef, lamb, Zinfandel, shallots, cilantro, parsley, mint, cumin, ginger, paprika, and cinnamon in a large bowl. Season with salt and pepper. Handling the meat as little as possible to avoid compacting it, mix well. Divide the mixture into 4 equal portions and form the portions into patties to fit the rolls.

● When the grill is ready, brush the grill rack with olive oil. Place the patties on the rack, cover, and cook, turning once, until done to preference, 5 to 7 minutes on each side for medium. During the last few minutes of cooking, place the rolls, cut side down, on the outer edges of the rack to toast lightly.

● To assemble the burgers, spread the aioli over the cut sides of the rolls. On each roll bottom, place a lettuce leaf, a patty, and an equal portion of the relish. Add the roll tops and serve. *Makes 4 burgers*

Indian Burgers
with Grilled Banana Raita

Garam Masala (optional)

1-inch piece of cinnamon stick

1 teaspoon cardamom seeds

½ teaspoon whole cloves

½ teaspoon black peppercorns

½ teaspoon cumin seed

¼ teaspoon ground nutmeg, or a small piece
   of a whole nutmeg

Grilled Banana Raita

Vegetable oil, for brushing on the grill rack

2 very firm bananas, peeled

½ teaspoon ground cumin

1 cup plain yogurt

1 teaspoon honey

¼ teaspoon salt

⅛ teaspoon freshly ground black pepper

Patties

1⅓ pounds ground lamb

2 tablespoons finely chopped cilantro

1 garlic clove, minced

1 teaspoon grated fresh ginger

½ teaspoon ground cumin

¼ teaspoon ground cayenne, or more to taste

¼ teaspoon salt

4 hamburger buns, split

16 cucumber slices

4 tomato slices

● If making the garam masala, place all of the ingredients in a small grinder (such as coffee grinder) and grind until fine, about 30 seconds. Measure out 1 teaspoon and store the remainder in a tightly covered container for another use.

● Prepare a medium-hot fire in a charcoal grill with a cover, or preheat a gas grill to medium-high.

● To make the raita, when the grill is ready, brush the grill rack with vegetable oil. Place the bananas on the grill and cook, turning carefully, until lightly browned all over, 1 to 2 minutes. While the bananas are cooking, place the 1 teaspoon garam masala and the cumin in a small fire-proof skillet and toast on the grill, shaking occasionally, until the spices begin to turn color and release their fragrance, about 2 minutes. Chop the grilled bananas into small pieces and combine with the yogurt, honey, salt, pepper, and toasted spices in a bowl. Stir well and set aside.

● To make the patties, combine the lamb, cilantro, garlic, ginger, cumin, cayenne, and salt in a large bowl. Handling the meat as little as possible to avoid compacting it, mix well. Divide the mixture into 4 equal portions and form the portions into patties to fit the buns.

● Place the patties on the grill rack, cover, and cook, turning once, until done to preference, about 4 minutes on each side for medium-rare. During the last few minutes of cooking, place the buns, cut side down, on the outer edges of the rack to toast lightly.

● To assemble the burgers, on each bun bottom, place 4 cucumber slices, a tomato slice, a patty, and an equal portion of the raita. Add the bun tops and serve. *Makes 4 burgers*

Winner

Julie Winter
Grosse Pointe Park,
Michigan

Prize

Award for Creativity, 1996

**Chef Starr's
Wine Pairing**

Merlot

Retired educator Susan Asanovic regrets missing the thrill of hearing her name announced as

the winner of BBB, as there was no cook-off for the 1997 competition. (I prepared the top recipes

in my test kitchen and chose the prizewinners.) She did, however, participate as a finalist in 1993,

and remembers the "hot sun, great wine, and helpful competitors. The eleven other burger

meisters were helpful and friendly. The Sutter Home staff was extremely hospitable and the Inn

was lovely. Overall: unforgettable!"

Winner
Susan Asanovic
Wilton, Connecticut

Prize
Grand Prize, 1997

**Chef Starr's
Wine Pairing**
Zinfandel

Recipe Inspiration
"A trip to Sicily
inspired my burger
creation. I loved the
foods of the region,
and the wine."

Siciliano Burgers with Fresh Ciliegine and Sweet Tomato Butter

Sweet Tomato Butter

¾ cup sun-dried tomatoes packed in olive oil

2 tablespoons oil from sun-dried tomatoes

1 teaspoon mild honey

½ cup red flame seedless grapes (substitute green grapes, if necessary)

2 tablespoons plus one teaspoon brine-packed capers, rinsed and drained

½ cup fresh flat-leaf parsley leaves, chopped

Salt

Freshly ground black pepper

Patties

1 pound ground veal

¾ pound ground beef

4 garlic cloves, minced

½ cup fresh Italian bread crumbs

¼ cup pine nuts

1 teaspoon ground cinnamon

Large pinch of ground cayenne

1 teaspoon dried rosemary, ground in spice grinder

1 teaspoon kosher salt, or more to taste

Freshly ground black pepper

6 ciliegine (⅓-ounce fresh mozzarella cheese balls)

Vegetable oil, for brushing on the grill rack

12 radicchio leaves, trimmed to fit the bread

Oil from sun-dried tomatoes, for brushing on the radicchio

6 (3 by 4-inch) pieces Italian bread, preferably rosemary-semolina bread, halved lengthwise

- Prepare a medium-hot fire in a charcoal grill with a cover, or preheat a gas grill to medium-high.

- To make the tomato butter, combine the tomatoes, oil, honey, and grapes in a food processor and process to a paste. Transfer to a bowl and stir in the capers and parsley. Season to taste with salt and pepper. Set aside.

- To make the patties, combine the veal, beef, garlic, bread crumbs, nuts, cinnamon, cayenne, and rosemary in a large bowl and season with salt and pepper. Handling the meat as little as possible to avoid compacting it, mix well. Divide the mixture into 6 equal portions and flatten into 6 disks. Place 1 ciliegine in the center of each disk, then bring up the meat to enclose the cheese in the middle. Form into six patties to fit the bread sections.

- When the grill is ready, brush the grill rack with vegetable oil. Place the patties on the rack, cover, and cook, turning once, until done to preference, 5 to 7 minutes on each side for medium. Meanwhile, brush the radicchio lightly with tomato oil and grill until charred but still crisp, about 4 minutes. During the last few minutes of cooking, place the bread, cut side down, on the outer edges of the rack to toast lightly.

- To assemble the burgers, spread the tomato butter over the cut sides of the bread. On each bread bottom, place a radicchio leaf, a patty, and another radicchio leaf. Add the bread tops and serve. ***Makes 6 burgers***

Jamaican Me Crazy Burgers

Coconut Mayonnaise

1/2 cup mayonnaise

2 tablespoons unsweetened shredded coconut

1 tablespoon chopped macadamia nuts

1 tablespoon chopped cilantro

Just Ducky Banana Chutney

1/3 cup bottled duck sauce

1/3 cup prepared salsa

1 large banana, chopped

2 plum tomatoes, chopped

Patties

1 1/2 pounds ground beef

2 tablespoons chopped green bell pepper

2 tablespoons chopped green onion

1 tablespoon soy sauce

2 teaspoons ground allspice

1/2 teaspoon crumbled dried thyme

1/2 teaspoon ground cayenne

Vegetable oil, for brushing on the grill rack

6 Kaiser rolls, split

3 cups watercress, chopped

● Prepare a medium-hot fire in a charcoal grill with a cover, or preheat a gas grill to medium-high.

● To make the mayonnaise, combine all of the ingredients in a small bowl and stir until well combined. Cover and refrigerate until serving.

● To make the chutney, combine the duck sauce, salsa, and banana in an 8-inch fire-proof skillet. Place on the grill rack and cook, stirring, until thickened, about 5 minutes. Remove from the heat, stir in the chopped tomatoes, cover, and refrigerate until serving.

● To make the patties, combine the beef, bell pepper, green onion, soy sauce, allspice, thyme, and cayenne in a large bowl. Handling the meat as little as possible to avoid compacting it, mix well. Divide the mixture into 6 equal portions and form the portions into patties to fit the rolls.

● When the grill is ready, brush the grill rack with vegetable oil. Place the patties on the rack, cover, and cook, turning once, until done to preference, 5 to 7 minutes on each side for medium. During the last few minutes of cooking, place the rolls, cut side down, on the outer edges of the rack to toast lightly.

● To assemble the burgers, spread the mayonnaise over the cut sides of the roll tops. On each roll bottom, place 1/2 cup of the watercress, a patty, and an equal portion of the chutney. Add the roll tops and serve. *Makes 6 burgers*

Winner

Mary Lou Newhouse
South Burlington, Vermont

Prize

First Prize, 1997

**Chef Starr's
Wine Pairing**

White Merlot

Winner
Gloria Piantek
Skillman, New Jersey

Prize
Second Prize, 1997

**Chef Starr's
Wine Pairing**
Gewürztraminer

Cubana Pork Burgers

Cuban Pickle Salsa

1/2 cup cooked or canned black beans, rinsed
and drained

1/4 cup chopped dill pickles

1/4 cup chopped sweet pickles

1/3 cup chopped red onion

2 tablespoons freshly squeezed lime juice

2 tablespoons chopped cilantro

Spicy Mustard Spread

1/4 cup mayonnaise

3/4 tablespoon spicy brown mustard

Patties

1/2 pound lean smoked ham

1/2 cup cooked or canned black beans, rinsed
and drained

1 to 2 dried chipotle chiles, softened in hot
water and seeds removed

1 garlic clove, minced

1/2 pound ground pork

1 teaspoon chile powder

1/2 teaspoon ground cumin

1/8 teaspoon salt, or to taste

Vegetable oil, for brushing on the grill rack

4 crisp-crust round buns, split

3 ounces sliced Monterey Jack cheese

4 Bibb lettuce leaves

● Prepare a medium-hot fire in a charcoal grill with a cover, or preheat a gas grill to medium-high.

● To make the salsa, combine all of the ingredients in a bowl and mix well. Cover and refrigerate until serving.

● To make the spread, combine the mayonnaise and mustard in a small bowl and blend well. Cover and refrigerate until serving.

● To make the patties, chop the ham in a food processor. Add the beans, chiles, and garlic and process until finely chopped. Transfer to a large bowl and add the pork, chile powder, cumin, and salt. Handling the meat as little as possible to avoid compacting it, mix well. Divide the mixture into 4 equal portions and form the portions into patties to fit the buns.

● When the grill is ready, brush the grill rack with vegetable oil. Place the patties on the rack, cover, and cook, turning once, until done to preference, 4 to 5 minutes on each side for medium. During the last few minutes of cooking, place the buns, cut side down, on the outer edges of the rack to toast lightly. During the last 2 minutes of cooking, top the patties with the cheese to melt.

● To assemble the burgers, spread the mustard mixture over the cut sides of the bun tops. On each bun bottom, spread a layer of salsa and then top with a lettuce leaf, a patty, and more salsa. Add the bun tops and serve. *Makes 4 burgers*

Larry Elder was a vice president of sales and marketing for a technology training and business consulting

company when he won the BBB cook-off. Now owner of Elder Art Gallery, Larry recalls the contest as

"one of the most exciting moments in my cooking history. The setting on the lawn of the winery was

magnificent and the competition was keen. Each contestant had constructed very creative recipes and

I was sure that mine would be considered too simple to win a prize. This feeling of inadequacy coupled

with a strict time schedule for completion of the recipe added to my stress level. I was completely taken

by surprise when I was announced the winner. It was truly an exhilarating experience."

1998

Winner

Larry Elder
Charlotte, North Carolina

Prize

Grand Prize, 1998

**Chef Starr's
Wine Pairing**

Zinfandel

Recipe Inspiration

"The southeastern region
of the United States has
carried on a love affair with
barbecue pork for many
years. My favorite barbecue
flavors are those that incorporate vinegar and spices.
The recipe I created includes
pork and many other
ingredients which are typical
of the Carolina barbecue."

Carolina Pork Barbecue Burgers

Carolina Coleslaw

3 cups finely shredded green cabbage

½ cup julienned red and/or green bell pepper

2 green onions, chopped

2 tablespoons mayonnaise

2 tablespoons Sauvignon Blanc

2 teaspoons sugar

Salt

Freshly ground black pepper

Barbecue Burger Balm

½ cup molasses

⅓ cup apple cider vinegar

¼ cup spicy brown mustard

2 garlic cloves, minced

¼ teaspoon ground cayenne

Salt

Freshly ground black pepper

Patties

1½ pounds ground pork

¼ cup finely chopped red onion

1 teaspoon Paul Prudhomme Meat Magic
 Seasoning Blend or other meat seasoning
 blend

Vegetable oil, for brushing on the grill rack

4 seeded hamburger buns, split

● To make the coleslaw, combine the cabbage, pepper, and onions in a large bowl and toss well. Combine the mayonnaise, Sauvignon Blanc, sugar, and salt and pepper to taste in a small bowl and stir until well blended. Pour over the cabbage mixture, tossing to blend. Cover and refrigerate until serving.

● To make the balm, combine all of the ingredients, including salt and pepper to taste, in a small bowl. Stir to blend well and set aside.

● Prepare a medium-hot fire in a charcoal grill with a cover, or preheat a gas grill to medium-high.

● To make the patties, combine ¼ cup of the balm, the pork, onion, and seasoning blend in a large bowl. Handling the meat as little as possible to avoid compacting it, mix well. Divide the mixture into 4 equal portions and form the portions into patties to fit the buns.

● When the grill is ready, brush the grill rack with vegetable oil. Place the patties on the rack, cover, and cook, turning once and basting with the remaining balm, until done to preference, 4 to 5 minutes on each side for medium. During the last few minutes of cooking, place the buns, cut side down, on the outer edges of the rack to toast lightly.

● To assemble the burgers, on each bun bottom, place a patty and an equal portion of the coleslaw. Add the bun tops and serve. *Makes 4 burgers*

Caesar Salad and Flank Steak Burgers with Garlic Crostini

Dressing

2 tablespoons olive oil

1 tablespoon extra virgin olive oil

1½ teaspoons red wine vinegar

¾ teaspoon balsamic vinegar

⅛ teaspoon kosher salt

2 flat anchovy fillets packed in oil,
   drained and chopped

2 garlic cloves, chopped

2 teaspoons freshly squeezed lemon juice

¼ teaspoon chopped fresh flat-leaf parsley

Patties

1½ pounds ground flank steak

½ cup chopped fresh flat-leaf parsley

2 shallots, minced

3 garlic cloves, minced

3 tablespoons Zinfandel

1 teaspoon kosher salt

½ teaspoon lemon pepper seasoning

½ teaspoon freshly ground black pepper

Olive oil, for brushing on the grill rack

Garlic Crostini

8 (½-inch-thick) sourdough bread slices

Extra virgin olive oil, for brushing on the bread

4 garlic cloves, peeled and halved

1½ cups washed, dried, and shredded
   romaine lettuce

Shredded, freshly grated, or shaved
   Parmesan cheese to taste

● Prepare a medium-hot fire in a charcoal grill with a cover, or preheat a gas grill to medium-high.

● To make the dressing, combine the olive oils, vinegars, and salt in a small jar with a lid and shake until well blended. Mash the anchovy fillets and garlic together on a cutting board until they form a paste; transfer to a bowl. Add the oil and vinegar mixture, lemon juice, and parsley and whisk until smooth. Set aside.

● To make the patties, combine the steak, parsley, shallots, garlic, Zinfandel, salt, lemon pepper seasoning, and pepper in a large bowl. Handling the meat as little as possible to avoid compacting it, mix well. Divide the mixture into 4 equal portions and form the portions into patties to fit the bread slices.

● When the grill is ready, brush the grill rack with olive oil. Place the patties on the rack, cover, and cook, turning once, until done to preference, 5 to 7 minutes on each side for medium. During the last few minutes of cooking, to make the crostini, brush the bread slices to taste with olive oil on both sides. Place the bread slices on the outer edges of the rack, turning once, to toast lightly. Remove and rub each side of the toast with ½ garlic clove.

● To assemble the burgers, combine the lettuce and the dressing in a large bowl and toss lightly. On 4 of the bread slices, place an equal portion of the salad, a patty, and a generous sprinkling of Parmesan cheese. Top with the remaining slices and serve. *Makes 4 burgers*

Winner

Jason Boulanger

Williston, Vermont

Prize

First Prize, 1998

**Chef Starr's
Wine Pairing**

Sauvignon Blanc

Samurai Burgers

Patties

1½ pounds sushi-grade ahi tuna, ground

1 tablespoon minced fresh ginger

1 tablespoon minced fresh chives

3 garlic cloves, minced

2 tablespoons Sauvignon Blanc

1 tablespoon unseasoned rice vinegar

2 teaspoons Asian sesame oil

¼ teaspoon freshly ground black pepper

Sweet Ginger Sauce

½ cup plum jam

5 tablespoons grated fresh ginger

¾ cup dashi (Japanese fish broth)

2 tablespoons soy sauce

2 tablespoons Moscato

¼ cup Dijon mustard

1 cup julienned daikon radish

1 sheet toasted nori, cut into fine shreds

1 cup sunflower sprouts

Vegetable oil, for brushing on the grill rack

4 sesame seed sandwich buns, split

- Prepare a medium-hot fire in a charcoal grill with a cover, or preheat a gas grill to medium-high.

- To make the patties, combine the tuna, ginger, chives, garlic, Sauvignon Blanc, rice vinegar, sesame oil, and pepper in a large bowl. Handling the tuna as little as possible to avoid compacting it, mix well. Divide the mixture into 4 equal portions and form the portions into patties to fit the buns. Cover and refrigerate until ready to cook.

- To make the sauce, combine the plum jam, ginger, dashi, soy sauce, and Moscato in a small saucepan. Place on the grill and bring the mixture to a boil. Add the mustard and cook, stirring constantly, for 1 minute. Remove from the heat and set aside.

- Combine the daikon, nori, and sunflower sprouts in a bowl and toss gently. Set aside.

- When the grill is ready, brush the grill rack with vegetable oil. Place the patties on the rack, cover, and cook, turning once, just until opaque throughout, about 2 minutes on each side for medium. During the last few minutes of cooking, place the buns, cut side down, on the outer edges of the rack to toast lightly.

- To assemble the burgers, spread the sauce over the cut sides of the bun bottoms. On each bun bottom, place a patty and an equal portion of the daikon mixture. Add the bun tops and serve. *Makes 4 burgers*

Sauerbraten Burgers

Sour-Cream-and-Dill Horseradish Topping

1 (8-ounce) container sour cream

2 tablespoons chopped fresh dill

1 tablespoon prepared horseradish

1 tablespoon mayonnaise

Wine Basting Sauce

¼ cup Zinfandel

¼ cup dill pickle juice

¼ cup liquid from canned sauerkraut

½ teaspoon ground cloves

½ teaspoon ground ginger

½ teaspoon instant espresso powder

Patties

2 pounds ground beef

½ cup finely crushed gingersnaps

½ cup finely chopped onion

½ cup finely chopped dill pickle

1 (8-ounce) can sauerkraut, drained and
squeezed dry; reserve ¼ cup liquid for
basting sauce

2 tablespoons spicy brown mustard

1 tablespoon Paul Prudhomme's Meat Magic
Seasoning Blend or other meat seasoning
blend

1 teaspoon grated lemon zest

1 teaspoon ground ginger

1 teaspoon celery seed

Vegetable oil, for brushing on the grill rack

16 dark rye bread slices

8 slices Muenster cheese with caraway seeds

8 large red leaf lettuce leaves

16 tomato slices

16 red onion slices

● Prepare a medium-hot fire in a charcoal grill with a cover, or preheat a gas grill to medium-high.

● To make the topping, combine all of the ingredients in a small bowl and stir well. Cover and refrigerate until serving.

● To make the basting sauce, combine all of the ingredients in a small bowl and stir well. Set aside.

● To make the patties, combine the beef, gingersnaps, onion, pickle, sauerkraut, mustard, seasoning blend, lemon zest, ginger, and celery seed in a large bowl. Handling the meat as little as possible to avoid compacting it, mix well. Divide the mixture into 8 equal portions and form the portions into patties to fit the bread slices.

● When the grill is ready, brush the grill rack with vegetable oil. Place the patties on the rack, cover, and cook, turning once, until done to preference, 5 to 7 minutes on each side for medium. During the last few minutes of cooking, place the bread slices on the outer edges of the rack, turning once, to toast lightly. During the last minute of cooking, place a cheese slice on top of each patty to melt.

● To assemble the burgers, spread one side of each bread slice with 1 tablespoon of the topping. On 8 of the slices, place a lettuce leaf, 2 tomato slices, 2 onion slices, and a patty. Add the remaining bread slices and serve. *Makes 8 burgers*

Winner
Debbie Vanni
Libertyville, Illinois

Prize
Award for Creativity, 1998

**Chef Starr's
Wine Pairing**
Gewürztraminer

With hundreds of wins from large to small under her apron strings, perhaps no one has won more

cooking prizes than Julie DeMatteo. The ex–school teacher, who now works part-time in a real

estate appraisal office, praises BBB as "one of the best cook-off experiences ever. Everything

was first-class and everyone was so gracious, accommodating, and just plain nice. I was also very

honored to win, considering the caliber of judges that year, including Chef Thomas Keller of the

famed French Laundry."

1999

Winner

Julie DeMatteo

Clemton, New Jersey

Prize

Grand Prize, 1999

Chef Starr's
Wine Pairing

Sauvignon Blanc

Recipe Inspiration

"My inspiration came
from my fondness
for Caribbean flavors.
I have always loved
the Jamaican blend
of spices, and thought
it would be good
with pork. The mango
mayo added a little
sweet balance."

Down Island Burgers with Mango Mayo & Grilled Onions

Mango Mayo

¼ cup mayonnaise

½ cup diced ripe mango

2 teaspoons freshly squeezed lime juice

Patties

1½ pounds ground pork

2 tablespoons Sauvignon Blanc

2 tablespoons TABASCO Pepper Sauce

¼ cup panko (Japanese bread crumbs)

4 large garlic cloves, minced

4 teaspoons minced fresh ginger

4 teaspoons curry powder

1 teaspoon salt

½ teaspoon ground allspice

Vegetable oil, for brushing on the grill rack

4 (½-inch-thick) sweet onion slices

4 seeded sandwich rolls, split

1 bunch watercress, large stems discarded

• Prepare a medium-hot fire in a charcoal grill with a cover, or preheat a gas grill to medium-high.

• To make the mayo, combine all of the ingredients in a food processor and process until smooth.

• To make the patties, combine the pork, Sauvignon Blanc, pepper sauce, panko, garlic, ginger, curry powder, salt, and allspice in a large bowl. Handling the meat as little as possible to avoid compacting it, mix well. Divide the mixture into 4 equal portions and form the portions into patties to fit the rolls.

• When the grill is ready, brush the grill rack with vegetable oil. Place the patties on the rack, cover, and cook, turning once, until done to preference, 4 to 5 minutes on each side for medium. While the patties are cooking, place the onions on the grill rack and cook until golden brown and crisp-tender, 2 to 3 minutes per side. During the last few minutes of cooking, place the rolls, cut side down, on the outer edges of the rack to toast lightly.

• To assemble the burgers, on each roll bottom, place a patty, an equal portion of the mayo, an onion slice, and a generous amount of watercress. Add the roll tops and serve.

Makes 4 burgers

Jamie Miller limits her work as a wine sales consultant to part time, so there's plenty of time for

contesting. Her creative efforts have paid off not only by winning BBB, as she's grabbed numerous prizes,

including Grand Prizes in Florida's Natural Citrus Recipe Cooking Contest and Campbell's Soup Contest,

and she placed just behind Kristine Snyder (page 116) at the 2003 National Chicken Cooking Contest

cook-off. Evaluating BBB, Jamie writes, "I've been to many cook-offs and Sutter Home's was definitely

one of the classiest and most fun! I appreciated the wine tasting that started at 10 A.M.! Cooking without a

glass of wine in my hand is simply unheard of in my world!"

2000

Winner
Jamie Miller
Maple Grove, Minnesota

Prize
Grand Prize, 2000

**Chef Starr's
Wine Pairing**
Gewürztraminer

Recipe Inspiration
"My love of
fresh tuna and
Asian/Hawaiian
ingredients
inspired my
winning burger."

Hawaiian Tuna Burgers with Maui Wowee Salsa

Maui Wowee Salsa

2 cups chopped Maui onion (or other
   sweet onion)

1/2 cup minced green onions

1/4 cup pickled ginger, chopped

1/4 cup cilantro, chopped

2 tablespoons Asian sesame oil

1 1/2 tablespoons soy sauce

1 tablespoon freshly squeezed lime juice

Patties

2 pounds boneless, skinless yellowfin tuna,
   finely chopped

1/2 cup panko (Japanese bread crumbs)

1 egg, lightly beaten

1/4 cup Dijon mustard

2 tablespoons minced garlic

2 tablespoons honey

1 1/2 tablespoons Asian sesame oil

2 teaspoons kosher salt

1/2 teaspoon freshly ground black pepper

1/4 teaspoon ground cayenne

Vegetable oil, for brushing on the grill rack

6 sesame buns, split

1/2 cup bottled teriyaki sauce

● Prepare a medium-hot fire in a charcoal grill with a cover, or preheat a gas grill to medium-high.

● To make the salsa, combine all of the ingredients in a bowl and mix well. Set aside to allow the flavors to blend.

● To make the patties, combine the tuna, panko, egg, mustard, garlic, honey, sesame oil, salt, pepper, and cayenne in a large bowl. Handling the tuna as little as possible to avoid compacting it, mix well. Divide the mixture into 6 equal portions and form the portions into patties to fit the buns.

● When the grill is ready, brush the grill rack with vegetable oil. Place the patties on the rack, cover, and cook, turning once, just until opaque throughout, about 4 minutes on each side. During the last few minutes of cooking, place the buns, cut side down, on the outer edges of the rack to toast lightly.

● To assemble the burgers, brush the cut sides of the buns with the teriyaki sauce. On each bun bottom, place a patty and an equal portion of the salsa. Add the bun tops and serve.

Makes 6 burgers

A harpist on the island of Maui, Kristine Snyder chose to pay homage to the

tropical flavors of her Hawaiian paradise in her recipe. She recounts, "After

finding out the qualifications of the other contestants, I figured I had no

chance in winning, so I just decided to have fun. What a great party! (Especially since I had incorporated

drinking wine into my recipe!) I was also impressed that Sutter Home used chefs for judges.

No one understands food better than they do. The four-foot check is hanging in my laundry room, but my

biggest smiles come from the incredible ceramic trophy that sits in my kitchen. The trophy is the best I've

seen in *any* contest!" Kristine should know about other cooking contests, as she has won many in the last

few years, including the National Chicken Cooking Contest and the Maui Onion Festival, and has scored high

in the National Beef Cook-Off and the Pillsbury Bake-Off®.

2001

Winner

Kristine Snyder

Kihei, Hawaii

Prize

Grand Prize, 2001

**Chef Starr's
Wine Pairing**

Sauvignon Blanc

"My inspiration was
a recipe called Glazed
Seabass with Ginger
Butter Sauce, which
I had made using
salmon. I wanted to
do an ahi burger until
I found out Jamie
Miller had stolen my
idea the year before!"

Soy-Glazed Salmon Burgers with Ginger-Lime Aioli

Ginger-Lime Aioli

1/2 cup mayonnaise

2 tablespoons sour cream

2 garlic cloves, minced

2 teaspoons minced fresh ginger

1 tablespoon freshly squeezed lime juice

1/4 teaspoon salt

Soy Glaze

1/3 cup low-sodium soy sauce

3 tablespoons honey

1 tablespoon unseasoned rice vinegar

1 tablespoon cornstarch

1 tablespoon plus 1 glass chilled Sauvignon Blanc

Patties

1 egg

2 tablespoons sour cream

1 tablespoon freshly squeezed lime juice

1 teaspoon Asian hot chile sauce

1 1/4 pounds skinless salmon fillets, chopped finely

2 green onions, thinly sliced

2 tablespoons chopped fresh mint leaves

2/3 cup fresh bread crumbs

1 teaspoon salt

Vegetable oil, for forming the patties and
  brushing on the grill rack

4 sesame buns, split

1/2 cucumber, peeled, seeded, and julienned

• Prepare a medium-hot fire in a charcoal grill with a cover, or preheat a gas grill to medium-high.

• To make the aioli, combine all of the ingredients in a bowl and mix well. Reserve 2 tablespoons for the patties and cover and refrigerate the remainder until serving.

• To make the glaze, combine the soy sauce, honey, and rice vinegar in a small, heavy fireproof saucepan. Mix the cornstarch and 1 tablespoon Sauvignon Blanc in a small bowl until smooth and add to the soy mixture. Place on the grill rack and stir the mixture until it boils and thickens slightly, about 3 minutes. Meanwhile, sip the glass of Sauvignon Blanc, saving the remainder for grilling. Set the glaze aside.

• To make the patties, combine the 2 tablespoons aioli, the egg, sour cream, lime juice, and chile sauce in a large bowl and whisk to blend well. Add the salmon, onions, mint, bread crumbs, and salt. Handling the salmon as little as possible to avoid compacting it, mix well. Coat your hands with vegetable oil and divide the mixture into 4 equal patties.

• When the grill is ready, brush the grill rack with vegetable oil. Place the patties on the rack, cover, and cook until browned on the bottom, about 3 minutes. Recommence sipping the glass of Sauvignon Blanc. Turn the patties and brush the cooked side with soy glaze. Cook, turning and brushing frequently with the glaze, just until opaque throughout, 4 to 5 minutes longer. During the last few minutes of cooking, place the buns, cut side down, on the outer edges of the rack to toast lightly.

• To assemble the burgers, top each bun bottom with an equal portion of the cucumber strips, a patty, and an equal portion of the aioli. Add the bun tops and serve. ***Makes 4 burgers***

Tamarind-Glazed Thai Burgers

Tamarind Glaze

¼ cup plus 2 tablespoons tamarind paste

2 tablespoons maple syrup

1 tablespoon unseasoned rice vinegar

1 tablespoon Sauvignon Blanc

1 tablespoon freshly squeezed lime juice

2 garlic cloves, minced

1 tablespoon minced fresh ginger

1 teaspoon salt

¼ teaspoon freshly ground black pepper

Patties

1 pound ground pork

1 pound ground chicken (preferably half thigh
   meat and half breast meat, mixed)

6 green onions, white and pale green parts
   only, thinly sliced

4 teaspoons minced fresh ginger

2 garlic cloves, minced

2 tablespoons soy sauce

2 tablespoons Sauvignon Blanc

¼ cup chopped cilantro

¼ cup chopped fresh Thai basil

¼ cup chopped fresh mint

2 teaspoons minced lime zest

1 teaspoon salt

½ teaspoon freshly ground black pepper

2 tablespoons Asian sesame oil, for brushing on the grill rack and the patties

6 sesame hamburger buns, split

1 large bunch watercress or arugula

1 hothouse cucumber, thinly sliced

1 red bell pepper, thinly sliced crosswise into rings

● To make the glaze, mash the tamarind paste in a small bowl. Add the remaining glaze ingredients and mix well. Strain into another small bowl, gently pushing any thick paste and tamarind seeds against the strainer with a spoon or spatula to get as much paste as possible and to get a smooth consistency. Set aside.

● Prepare a medium-hot fire in a charcoal grill with a cover, or preheat a gas grill to medium-high.

● To make the patties, in a large bowl, combine the pork, chicken, green onions, ginger, garlic, soy sauce, and Sauvignon Blanc and mix gently with your hands or a spoon. Add the cilantro, basil, mint, lime zest, salt, and pepper. Handling the meat as little as possible to avoid compacting it, mix well. Divide the mixture into 6 equal portions and form the portions into patties to fit the buns.

● When the grill is ready, brush the grill rack with some of the sesame oil. Place the patties on the rack, cover, and cook until browned on the bottom, about 4 minutes, then turn over. Brush with the remaining sesame oil and then baste with the glaze. Continue cooking just until the juices run clear when patties are pierced in the center, about 4 minutes longer. During the last few minutes of cooking, place the buns, cut side down, on the outer edges of the rack to toast lightly.

● To assemble the burgers, on each bun bottom, place some watercress, a patty, a little bit of the glaze, several cucumber slices, and a pepper ring. Add the bun tops and serve.

Makes 6 burgers

Winner

Norma Molitor

Austin, Texas

Prize

People's Choice Award

2001

Chef Starr's
Wine Pairing

Sauvignon Blanc

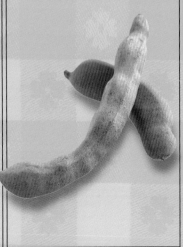

When Annelle Williams takes a break from her duties as a pharmacist, she's most likely to think

of cooking Italian fare. Annelle used her $20,000 prize to take a very memorable trip to Tuscany,

but that was just "the icing on the cake. Our trip to St. Helena and the new friends we made were

the real 'prizes' and ones we'll never forget. I've been a Burger Queen ever since, cooking that

burger all over town for every kind of fundraiser you can think of, so the fun has continued!"

2002

Winner

Annelle Williams
Martinsville, Virginia

Prize

Grand Prize, 2002

**Chef Starr's
Wine Pairing**

Shiraz (Syrah)

Recipe Inspiration

"The meat filling I use for
cannelloni is so delicious
that I was looking for a
way to incorporate it into
another recipe. For the
burger contest, I adjusted
the ingredients and added
two other favorite
things—grilled focaccia
for the bun and a
modified caprese salad
for the condiment."

Vitello Focaccia

Caprese Topping

12 tomato slices

12 fresh basil leaves

6 slices fresh mozzarella cheese

6 tablespoons olive oil

2 tablespoons balsamic vinegar

1 tablespoon Dijon mustard

1½ tablespoons dried Italian seasoning
    herb blend

½ teaspoon freshly ground black pepper

Patties

1 tablespoon olive oil

½ sweet yellow onion, chopped

1½ garlic cloves, chopped

2 ounces hard salami, cubed

2 ounces prosciutto, sliced

½ cup grated Parmesan cheese

2 tablespoons chopped fresh flat-leaf parsley

1½ pounds ground veal

1 egg, beaten

2 tablespoons Sauvignon Blanc

Vegetable oil, for brushing on the grill rack

6 bun-sized focaccia bread sections, sliced
    horizontally

2 tablespoons butter, melted

- Prepare a medium-hot fire in a charcoal grill with a cover, or preheat a gas grill to medium-high.

- To make the topping, combine the tomatoes, basil, and mozzarella in a shallow bowl. Combine the oil, vinegar, and mustard in a small bowl and whisk to blend well. Add the herb blend and pepper and whisk again. Pour the mixture over the tomato mixture and set aside to marinate.

- To make the patties, heat the olive oil in a small fire-proof skillet on the grill rack. Add the onion and garlic and sauté until soft, about 5 minutes. Remove from the heat and set aside.

- Combine the salami, prosciutto, Parmesan, and parsley in a food processor and process just until coarsely ground. Transfer the mixture to a large bowl and add the veal, onion mixture, egg, and Sauvignon Blanc. Handling the meat as little as possible to avoid compacting it, mix well. Divide the mixture into 6 equal portions and form the portions into patties to fit the focaccia sections.

- When the grill is ready, brush the grill rack with vegetable oil. Place the patties on the rack, cover, and cook, turning once, just until done to preference, 3 to 5 minutes on each side for medium. Remove from the heat and let rest while grilling the bread. Brush the cut sides of the focaccia with the butter and place, cut side down, on the outer edges of the rack to toast lightly.

- To assemble the burgers, remove the tomatoes, basil, and mozzarella from the marinade. On each bottom focaccia, place a veal patty, 2 tomato slices, 2 basil leaves, and a slice of mozzarella. Add the focaccia tops and serve. *Makes 6 burgers*

Spicy Summer Shrimp Burgers with Crisp Pancetta

Patties

2 teaspoons kosher or coarse sea salt

1/2 teaspoon freshly ground black pepper

1 tablespoon prepared horseradish

1 1/2 cups fresh corn kernels, including "milk" from scraping the cobs with the back of a knife

2 pounds raw shrimp (any size), peeled, deveined, and coarsely chopped

3 tablespoons minced sun-dried tomatoes packed in olive oil

1 tablespoon minced fresh tarragon

Chile Mayonnaise

1/2 cup mayonnaise

2 tablespoons bottled chile sauce

Kosher or coarse sea salt

Freshly ground black pepper

6 thinly sliced rounds of pancetta or other bacon

Grapeseed or other flavorless oil, for brushing on the patties and the grill rack

6 challa or egg bread rolls, split

Unsalted butter, for spreading on the rolls

6 beefsteak tomato slices

12 thin avocado slices (peel and slice at last minute to prevent from turning brown)

Salt

Freshly ground black pepper

6 butter lettuce leaves, washed and dried

• To make the patties, combine the salt, pepper, horseradish, and 3/4 cup of the corn in a food processor and process until fairly smooth. Add one-third of the shrimp and blend until smooth. Transfer the mixture to a large, chilled bowl. Fold in the remaining 3/4 cup of the corn, the remaining chopped shrimp, sun-dried tomatoes, and tarragon. Handling the shrimp as little as possible to avoid compacting it, mix well. Divide the mixture into 6 equal portions and form the portions into patties to fit the rolls. Cover and refrigerate for 30 minutes or up to 2 hours. Remove from the refrigerator about 15 minutes before grilling.

• Prepare a medium-hot fire in a charcoal grill with a cover, or preheat a gas grill to medium-high.

• To make the chile mayonnaise, combine the mayonnaise, chile sauce, and salt and pepper to taste in a small bowl and whisk to blend well. Cover and refrigerate until serving.

• When the grill is ready, place a cast-iron or other heavy-duty fire-proof skillet on the grill rack and cook the pancetta until golden brown and crisp; drain on paper towels.

• Generously brush both sides of the chilled patties and the grill rack with oil. Place the patties on the rack, cover, and cook, turning very carefully once, just until opaque throughout, about 5 minutes on each side. During the last few minutes of cooking, spread the cut sides of the rolls with butter and place, cut side down, on the outer edges of the rack to toast lightly.

• Sprinkle the tomato and avocado slices with salt and pepper to taste.

• To assemble the burgers, spread the mayonnaise over the cut sides of the rolls. On each roll bottom, place a lettuce leaf, a tomato slice, 2 avocado slices, a patty, and a pancetta slice. Add the roll tops and serve. *Makes 6 burgers*

Winner

Adam Payson

Omaha, Nebraska

Prize

People's Choice Award,
2002

**Chef Starr's
Wine Pairing**

Shiraz (Syrah)

Chipotle-Honey BBQ Bacon Burgers with Gorgonzola Cheese

Patties

1½ pounds ground beef

4 ounces ground pork sausage

¼ cup sliced green onion

2 tablespoons diced red bell pepper

1 tablespoon minced garlic

2 tablespoons freshly ground black pepper

Chipotle-Honey BBQ Sauce

2 tablespoons olive oil

¼ cup diced red onion

2 canned chipotle chiles in adobo sauce,
   chopped

2 tablespoons diced green bell pepper

2 tablespoons diced red bell pepper

2 tablespoons diced Roma tomato

3 tablespoons minced garlic

1 cup apple cider vinegar

1 tablespoon dry mustard

1 cup ketchup

½ cup honey

8 thick peppered bacon slices

Vegetable oil, for brushing on the grill rack

4 (5-inch) Kaiser rolls, split

4 ounces Gorgonzola cheese, crumbled

8 (¼-inch-thick) Roma tomato slices

- Prepare a medium-hot fire in a charcoal grill with a cover, or preheat a gas grill to medium-high.

- To make the patties, combine the beef, pork, green onion, bell pepper, and garlic in a large bowl. Handling the meat as little as possible to avoid compacting it, mix well. Divide the mixture into 4 equal portions and form the portions into patties to fit the rolls. Coat with the black pepper. Refrigerate until needed.

- To make the sauce, when the grill is ready, heat the olive oil in a 2-quart fire-proof saucepan on the grill rack. Add the onion, chiles, bell peppers, tomato, and garlic and sauté until soft, about 5 minutes. Deglaze with the vinegar and let simmer. Add the mustard and blend until smooth. Stir in the ketchup and honey and bring to a slow simmer.

- Cook the bacon until crisp in a fire-proof griddle or frying pan on the grill rack. Keep warm for later use.

- Brush the grill rack with vegetable oil. Place the patties on the rack, cover, and cook, turning once and basting frequently with the sauce, until done to preference, 5 to 7 minutes on each side for medium. During the last few minutes of cooking, place the rolls, cut side down, on the outer edges of the rack to toast lightly.

- To assemble the burgers, spread 1 teaspoon of the sauce over the cut sides of each roll. On each roll bottom, place 1 ounce of the cheese, 2 bacon slices, a patty, and 2 tomato slices. Add the roll tops and serve. *Makes 4 burgers*

Classical soprano Susan Mello hit the high note with her Greek-inspired burgers. She remembers:

"I absolutely loved participating in BBB for two consecutive years. Every aspect of the competition

was not only professional, but the staff was a joy to be around. The fact that all of the proceeds

went to breast-cancer research both years made me very proud to be a part of this event. BBB

was my first win and the only competition I had entered. I am now 'hooked' and regularly enter

contests with new recipes that I create."

2003

Winner

Susan Mello
Jackson Heights, New York

Prize

Grand Prize, 2003

**Chef Starr's
Wine Pairing**

Merlot

Recipe Inspiration

"For twelve years, I
lived in Astoria, Queens,
which has the largest
Greek population outside
of Athens. I would eat
Greek food all the time
and thought it would be
a neat idea to combine
all of my favorite Greek
cuisine in a burger."

My Big Fat Greco-Inspired Burgers

Tzatziki with Feta

1 small cucumber, peeled, seeded, and
    chopped

1½ cups plain yogurt

1 garlic clove, minced

3 tablespoons finely chopped fresh dill

½ cup crumbled Greek feta cheese

Grilled Eggplant

3 tablespoons white wine vinegar

½ teaspoon dried oregano

½ teaspoon salt

¼ teaspoon freshly ground black pepper

¼ cup olive oil

1 large eggplant, sliced into rounds
    ½ inch thick

Patties

2 pounds ground lamb

¾ cup chopped fresh mint leaves

1½ tablespoons ground cumin

Salt

Freshly ground black pepper

Vegetable oil, for brushing on the grill rack

6 small pita breads, halved horizontally

3 cups chopped romaine lettuce

- To make the tzatziki, combine all of the ingredients in a bowl and mix well. Cover and refrigerate for 1 hour.

- Prepare a medium-hot fire in a charcoal grill with a cover, or preheat a gas grill to medium-high.

- To make the grilled eggplant, combine the vinegar, oregano, salt, and pepper in a small bowl and then whisk in the olive oil until the mixture is thick and well blended. Arrange the eggplant slices in a 9 by 13-inch baking dish, pour the dressing over, and turn the eggplant to coat well. Set aside.

- To make the patties, combine the lamb, mint, and cumin in a large bowl and season with salt and pepper. Handling the meat as little as possible to avoid compacting it, mix well. Divide the mixture into 6 equal portions and form the portions into patties to fit the pita breads.

- When the grill is ready, brush the grill rack with vegetable oil. Place the patties on the rack, cover, and cook, turning once, just until done, about 4 minutes on each side for medium-rare. Grill the eggplant slices until tender, about 3 minutes on each side. During the last few minutes of cooking, place the pita breads, cut side down, on the outer edges of the rack to toast lightly.

- To assemble the burgers, on each bread bottom, place ½ cup lettuce, a patty, an equal portion of the tzatziki, and an eggplant slice. Add the bread tops and serve. ***Makes 6 burgers***

Andouille-Shrimp Burgers with Creole Honey Mustard

Creole Honey Mustard

3 tablespoons Dijon mustard

1½ tablespoons mayonnaise

1½ tablespoons honey

2 teaspoons mustard seed

2 teaspoons minced chives

2 dashes TABASCO Pepper Sauce

Patties

2 pounds pork shoulder (Boston butt)

6 ounces smoked bacon

3 large garlic cloves

2 tablespoons whole-grain mustard

1 tablespoon ground smoked paprika

1 tablespoon liquid smoke

1 teaspoon TABASCO Pepper Sauce

1 teaspoon onion powder

1½ teaspoons dried oregano

1 tablespoon kosher salt

1¼ pounds large shrimp, peeled and deveined

2 eggs

1 cup fresh bread crumbs

Grilled Onions

8 (¼-inch-thick) yellow onion slices

Olive oil, for brushing on the onions

Salt

Freshly ground black pepper

Vegetable oil, for brushing on the grill rack

8 sourdough Kaiser rolls, split

● To make the mustard, combine all of the ingredients in a small bowl and mix thoroughly. Cover and refrigerate until serving.

● To make the patties, cut the pork and bacon into 1-inch cubes and mix with the garlic, mustard, paprika, liquid smoke, pepper sauce, onion powder, oregano, and salt. Using a medium die, grind the mixture into a bowl, or finely chop in a food processor. Set aside for 30 to 45 minutes.

● Prepare a medium-hot fire in a charcoal grill with a cover, or preheat a gas grill to medium-high.

● Cut the shrimp into ¼-inch pieces and fold into the pork mixture. Add the eggs and bread crumbs. Handling the meat as little as possible to avoid compacting it, mix well. Divide the mixture into 8 equal portions and form the portions into patties to fit the rolls.

● To make the grilled onions, brush the onion slices with olive oil and season to taste with salt and pepper.

● When the grill is ready, brush the grill rack with vegetable oil. Place the onion slices on a cooler part of the rack, cover, and cook turning once, until very soft, 10 to 15 minutes. Place the patties on the rack, cover, and cook, turning once, until done to preference, 4 to 5 minutes on each side for medium. During the last few minutes of cooking, place the rolls, cut side down, on the outer edges of the rack to toast lightly.

● To assemble the burgers, on each roll bottom, place a patty, 1 tablespoon of the mustard, and a grilled onion slice. Add the roll tops and serve. *Makes 8 burgers*

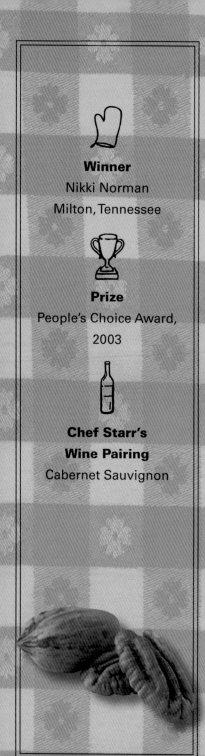

Winner
Nikki Norman
Milton, Tennessee

Prize
People's Choice Award,
2003

**Chef Starr's
Wine Pairing**
Cabernet Sauvignon

Buttered Pecan Buffalo Burgers with Cabernet Cranberries and Herbed Mayonnaise

Cabernet Cranberries

1 cup dried cranberries

⅔ cup Cabernet Sauvignon

Buttered Pecans

½ cup unsalted butter

1 cup pecan halves

1 teaspoon sea salt

Patties

1½ pounds ground buffalo

1 cup panko (Japanese bread crumbs)

¼ cup TABASCO Chipotle Pepper Sauce

1 tablespoon avocado oil

1 egg, lightly beaten

2 large garlic cloves, minced

1 teaspoon salt

1 teaspoon freshly ground Tellicherry pepper

Vegetable oil, for brushing on the grill rack

6 Kaiser rolls, split

6 slices Monterey Jack cheese

2 teaspoons Mrs. Dash Steak Grilling Blend
    or other meat grilling blend

¾ cup mayonnaise

2 Hass avocados

Juice of 1 lemon (optional)

6 red leaf lettuce leaves

• Prepare a medium-hot fire in a charcoal grill with a cover, or preheat a gas grill to medium-high.

• To make the Cabernet cranberries, combine the ingredients in a small bowl. Set aside.

• To make the buttered pecans, melt the butter in a small fire-proof skillet on the grill rack. Add the pecans and salt and sauté until the nuts are lightly browned, about 6 minutes. Remove from the heat and strain the pecans in a strainer, catching the butter in a small bowl. Transfer the pecans to a food processor and grind finely. Set the butter aside.

• To make the patties, combine the Cabernet cranberries (including the wine), the ground pecans, buffalo, panko, pepper sauce, avocado oil, egg, garlic, salt, and pepper in a large bowl. Handling the meat as little as possible to avoid compacting it, mix well. Divide the mixture into 6 equal portions and form the portions into patties to fit the rolls.

• When the grill is ready, brush the grill rack with vegetable oil. Place the patties on the rack, cover, and cook, turning once, until done to preference, 5 to 7 minutes on each side for medium. During the last few minutes of cooking, brush the cut sides of the rolls with the butter from cooking the pecans and place them, cut side down, on the outer edges of the rack to toast lightly. During the last 2 minutes of cooking, place the cheese on the patties to melt.

• While the burgers are cooking, combine the grilling blend and mayonnaise in a small bowl and mix well. Peel, pit, and slice the avocados into 18 slices; dip into the lemon juice if not using immediately.

• To assemble the burgers, spread the mayonnaise on the cut side of the roll tops. On each roll bottom, place a patty, a lettuce leaf, and 3 avocado slices. Add the roll tops and serve.

Makes 6 burgers

"You don't have to be a rocket scientist to win BBB, but it helps," proclaimed

Sutter Home president Bob Torkelson after Clint Stephenson, a mass-properties

engineer who calculates spacecraft centers of gravity, blasted off to victory with the competition's

first $50,000 Grand Prize. Explaining why his recipe is a great American burger, Clint stated, "Since

America is truly a melting pot of diverse races and cultures, the regional influences of our country are

evident in the way we prepare our burgers. My burger recipe is a tribute to the creative and trendsetting

cooks across the country who have been instrumental in reviving a culinary sense of pride in regional

American cooking. By combining fresh ingredients in a new and creative manner, I have developed an

incredible new burger with layers of flavor throughout. This burger *will rock your world!!!*"

2004

Winner

Clint Stephenson
Friendswood, Texas

Prize

Grand Prize, 2004

**Chef Starr's
Wine Pairing**

Zinfandel

Recipe Inspiration

"To commemorate the
100th birthday of the
hamburger in America,
I was inspired to create
this new recipe by
combining two all-time
favorites: burgers and
BLT sandwiches."

Grilled California Avocado BLT Burgers with Caramelized Chipotle Onions

Caramelized Chipotle Onions

1 large sweet onion, halved and thinly sliced

1 tablespoon TABASCO Chipotle Pepper Sauce

1 tablespoon beef broth

1 tablespoon balsamic vinegar

1 tablespoon olive oil

1 tablespoon minced fresh garlic

1 tablespoon dark brown sugar

Point Reyes Blue Cheese Spread

6½ ounces light garlic-and-herbs spreadable cheese

4 ounces Point Reyes blue cheese or other favorite blue cheese, crumbled

Patties

1 pound ground chuck

1 pound ground sirloin

⅓ cup minced sweet onion

¼ cup Zinfandel

3 tablespoons minced fresh oregano, thyme, and basil (any combination)

1 tablespoon TABASCO Chipotle Pepper Sauce

1½ teaspoons spicy seasoned salt

Vegetable oil, for brushing on the grill rack

12 Hass avocado slices

Balsamic vinegar, for brushing on the avocado

Spicy seasoned salt, for sprinkling on the avocado slices

12 precooked bacon slices

6 (4½-inch) soft Kaiser rolls, split

6 romaine lettuce leaves

6 (¼-inch-thick) large tomato slices

● Prepare a medium-hot fire in a charcoal grill with a cover, or preheat a gas grill to medium-high.

● To make the caramelized onions, combine the onion, pepper sauce, broth, vinegar, oil, garlic, and brown sugar in a 10-inch nonstick, fire-proof skillet, cover with a lid, and place on the grill rack. Cook the onion mixture for 15 to 20 minutes, stirring occasionally, until the onions are caramelized and most of the liquid is evaporated. Remove the pan from the grill and set aside.

● To make the spread, combine the cheeses in a fire-proof saucepan, cover, and set aside.

● To make the patties, combine the chuck, sirloin, onion, Zinfandel, herbs, pepper sauce, and seasoned salt in a large bowl. Handling the meat as little as possible to avoid compacting it, mix well. Divide the mixture into 6 equal portions and form the portions into patties to fit the rolls.

● Brush the grill rack with vegetable oil. Place the patties on the rack, cover, and cook, turning once, until done to preference, 5 to 7 minutes on each side for medium. Meanwhile, place the saucepan with the cheese spread on the outer edge of the rack to warm the cheese

(continued)

139

Grilled California Avocado BLT Burgers with Caramelized Chipotle Onions (continued)

mixture just until it reaches a very soft, spreadable consistency. Remove the saucepan from the grill and set aside.

- During the final minutes of grilling the patties, brush the avocado slices with balsamic vinegar and sprinkle with seasoned salt. Arrange on a rimmed nonstick perforated grilling pan coated lightly with oil and grill alongside the patties for 1 to 2 minutes, turning as necessary. During the final 30 seconds, add the bacon slices to the pan. When the avocados are nicely grilled and the bacon is crisp, remove from the grill. When the patties are cooked, remove from the grill, stacking to keep warm. Place the rolls, cut side down, on the outer edges of the grill rack to toast lightly.

- To assemble the burgers, spread a generous amount of the cheese mixture over the cut sides of the rolls. On each roll bottom, place a lettuce leaf, a tomato slice, a patty, an equal portion of the caramelized onions, 2 avocado slices, and 2 bacon slices. Add the roll tops and serve. *Makes 6 burgers*

the judges

Better Burger Judges

an impressive list of culinary professionals—chefs, cookbook authors, cooking teachers, editors, entrepreneurs, journalists, radio broadcasters, restaurant critics, and television cooking-show hosts—have accepted the invitation to judge the Build a Better Burger cook-off through the years. Thomas Keller of The French Laundry and Judy Rodgers of Zuni Cafe have received James Beard awards for best chef in America, and Mark Miller, Caprial Pence, and Chris Schlesinger have won Beard awards for best chef in their regions. A number of the cookbook authors have won awards from both the James Beard Foundation and the International Association of Culinary Professionals (IACP). Two presidents of the IACP joined us during their year in office. I think all of the judges who've contributed their time to the contest have enjoyed their relaxing weekend in Napa Valley along with the task of choosing the year's best burger. Several have kindly dubbed BBB as the best-organized cooking contest they've ever judged.

Here is a list of our esteemed judges to date. Following the list are recipes from some of the judges that illustrate our varied ideas of what makes a perfect burger. A few prefer to cook their patties on a stove, rather than on a grill as required for the contest.

James McNair, Head Judge (1990–2004) Author of more than forty cookbooks; Build a Better Burger National Cook-Off Chairman; cooking teacher; former food spokesperson for Sutter Home; book designer; food stylist and photographer; and recipient of the IACP Award of Excellence in Food Photography.

Bruce Aidells (2000) Founder of Aidells Sausage Company; author of numerous cookbooks, including the meat and poultry sections of the latest *Joy of Cooking*; and coauthor of *The Complete Meat Cookbook* and the IACP award–winning *Hot Links and Country Flavors.*

Antonia Allegra (1999 and 2004) Editor-in-chief of *Vine Napa Valley* magazine; Director of Symposium for Professional Food Writers at the Greenbrier and Symposium for Professional Wine Writers at Meadowood; past president of the IACP; founding editor of *Appellation* magazine; and author of *Napa Valley: The Ultimate Winery Guide* and *Napa Valley Expedition Guide* audio tour and guidebook.

Joey Altman (2002) Host of *Bay Cafe* on KRON-TV in San Francisco; recipient of two James Beard Awards for Best Local Cooking Show; former chef/owner of Wild Hare in Menlo Park, California; and former chef for Miss Pearl's Jam House, Stars, and several other restaurants and top caterers in San Francisco, and Commander's Palace in New Orleans under Chef Emeril Lagasse.

Pam Anderson (2002) Food columnist for *USA Weekend* magazine; author of *CookSmart, How to Cook without a Book,* and the IACP award–winning *The Perfect Recipe*; cooking teacher; food writer for *Fine Cooking, Cooking Light, Food & Wine, Saveur,* and other magazines; and former executive editor of *Cook's Illustrated* magazine and food editor of *Cook's* magazine.

Michael Bauer (1994) Executive food and wine editor of the *San Francisco Chronicle*; coeditor of *The San Francisco Chronicle Cookbook* and *The Secrets of Success Cookbook*; former restaurant critic and wine editor of the *Dallas Times Herald*; former features writer at the *Kansas City Star*; recipient of the Association of Food Journalists' top award for restaurant criticism; and an inductee into the James Beard Foundation's Who's Who of American Food and Beverage.

Jan Birnbaum (1995) Executive chef/owner of Catahoula Restaurant and Saloon in Calistoga, California, and former executive chef of Campton Place Hotel in San Francisco.

Anthony Dias Blue (1996) Wine and spirits editor of *Bon Appétit* magazine; director of the San Francisco Fair International Wine competition; and author of *American Wine— A Comprehensive Guide.*

Flo Braker (1996) Cooking teacher; columnist for the *San Francisco Chronicle* food section; author of *The Simple Art of Perfect Baking* and the IACP award–winning *Sweet Miniatures*; and past president of the IACP.

Kathleen Buckley (1991) European-based wine and travel writer for websites and publications; managing editor of the *Wine Enthusiast* magazine and website; and former lifestyle editor of the *Oakland Tribune.*

Gene Burns (1998) Host of the weekly *Dining Around with Gene Burns* and a nightly talk show on KGO radio in San Francisco, and former host of a nationally syndicated talk show originating on WOR in New York City.

L. Pierce Carson (2004) Food and wine editor and features writer for the *Napa Valley Register.*

Greg Cole (2001) Executive chef/owner of Celadon and Cole's Chop House in Napa, California, and former chef at Pasta Prego and Ristorante Piatti in Sonoma, California.

Elaine Corn (1991) Author of several cookbooks, including the James Beard Foundation and IACP award–winning *Now You're Cooking: Everything a Beginner Needs to Know to Start Cooking Today,* and former food editor of the *Sacramento Bee, Louisville Courier-Journal* and *Austin American-Statesman.*

Marion Cunningham (1993, 1994, and 2000) Author of *The Fannie Farmer Cookbook* (revised editions), *The Fannie Farmer Baking Book, The Breakfast Book,* and *The Supper Book;* food columnist for the *Los Angeles Times* and *San Francisco Chronicle;* restaurant and recipe consultant; former assistant to James Beard; and recipient of the James Beard Foundation's Lifetime Achievement Award.

David Duran (1995) Executive of H-E-B, Texas's largest supermarket chain.

Janet Fletcher (1998) Staff food and wine writer for the *San Francisco Chronicle;* author or coauthor of sixteen cookbooks, including *Fresh from the Farmers' Market* and *The Cheese Course;* and recipient of two James Beard Awards for Newspaper Feature Writing and an IACP Bert Green Award for food journalism.

Hugh Garvey (2003) Senior editor of *Bon Appétit* magazine and freelance writer for *Travel and Leisure, GQ, Details,* and *Fortune* magazines and the *Village Voice.*

Duncan Gott (2001) Co-owner of Taylor's Automatic Refresher, San Francisco and St. Helena, California.

Joel Gott (2001) Co-owner of Taylor's Automatic Refresher, San Francisco and St. Helena, California, and Napa Valley winemaker.

Fred Halpert (1995) Chef/owner of Brava Terrace in St. Helena, California.

Kate Heyhoe (2002) Executive editor of *Global Gourmet* (globalgourmet.com); author of *Cooking with Kids for Dummies* and *A Chicken in Every Pot;* coauthor of *Harvesting the Dream: The Rags to Riches Tale of the Sutter Home Winery;* and former chef/owner of a restaurant in Italy.

Martha Holmberg (2003) Publisher and former editor-in-chief of *Fine Cooking* magazine; former administrative director of La Varenne cooking school; former cookbook editor in London and Paris; and former private chef in Paris and cook at Mocha Cafe in Cherry Creek, Colorado.

Todd Humphries (2002) Executive chef/co-owner of Martini House in St. Helena, California; former executive chef of the Wine Spectator Greystone Restaurant in St. Helena and Campton Place Hotel in San Francisco; and former chef at the Peninsula Hotel and Lespinasse in New York City.

Philippe Jeanty (2001) Chef/owner of Bistro Jeanty and Père Jeanty in Yountville, California, and Jeanty at Jack's in San Francisco, and former executive chef of Domaine Chandon restaurant in Napa Valley.

Elaine Johnston (1991) editor in the food department of *Sunset* magazine and books; cooking teacher; and food writer for *British House and Garden* and *Taste* magazines and the *International Herald Tribune.*

Lynne Rosetto Kasper (1999) Author of *The Splendid Table,* the only book to that date to win Cookbook of the Year awards from both the James Beard Foundation and the IACP; host of *The Splendid Table* on National Public Radio, which received a James Beard Award for Best National Radio Show on Food; cooking teacher; and freelance food writer for the *New York Times, Washington Post, Los Angeles Times,* and *Food & Wine* and *Bon Appétit* magazines.

Thomas Keller (1999) Chef/owner of The French Laundry (often named the number one restaurant in America) and Bouchon bistro and bakery in Yountville, California, Bouchon in Las Vegas, and Per Se in New York City; author of *The French Laundry Cookbook,* an IACP Cookbook of the Year award winner; and recipient of James Beard Foundation Awards for Best Chef: California and America's Outstanding Chef of the Year.

Ellen Koteff (2003) Executive editor of the *Nation's Restaurant News*; recipient of the McAllister Editorial Fellowship from the American Business Media; and former newspaper writer in Parsippany, New Jersey, and Palm Beach, Florida.

Sheila Lukins (2000) Food editor of *Parade* magazine; coauthor of the *Silver Palate* cookbooks, including the IACP award–winning *Good Times Cookbook* and *The New Basics Cookbook*; and author of *All Around the World Cookbook, U.S.A. Cookbook,* and *Celebrate!*

Susan Mayo (1994) Vice president of consumer affairs for Farm Fresh markets in Virginia.

Kelly McCune (1990) Author of *The Art of Grilling* and the IACP award–winning *The Grill Book.*

Mark Miller (1994) Chef/owner of Coyote Cafe in Santa Fe, New Mexico, Red Sage in Washington, DC, and Wildfire in Sydney, Australia; author of eleven cookbooks, including *Coyote Cafe, Coyote Pantry,* and *The Great Chile Book*; former chef at Chez Panisse and chef/owner of Fourth Street Grill and the Santa Fe Bar and Grill in Berkeley, California; and recipient of a James Beard Award for Best Chef: Southwest.

Krista Montgomery (2003) Food editor of *Cooking Light* magazine and former food editor for *Gusto!*, a Latin edition of *Cooking Light.*

Jeff Morgan (2004) Author of *The Dean and Deluca Cookbook*; coauthor of *The Working Parents Cookbook*; wine writer; winemaker; and former East Coast editor for *Wine Spectator* magazine.

Jodi Morgan (2004) Coauthor of *The Working Parents Cookbook* and executive director of the American Institute of Wine and Food.

Lori Lyn Narlock (2004) Author of *The Food Lover's Companion to Napa Valley*; coauthor of *Smoothies* and *Cocktail Food*; food columnist for the *Napa Valley Register*; and event coordinator of the 1993 Build a Better Burger contest.

Charles Neave (2002) Editor of *Destination Napa Valley*; writer for *Esquire, Yankee,* the *Boston Globe,* and other magazines and newspapers; and coauthor of *Uncle Billy's Downeast Barbeque Book.*

Katie O'Kennedy (2002) Senior editor of *Bon Appétit* magazine.

Cindy Pawlcyn (1995 and 2001) Executive chef/owner of Cindy's Backstreet Kitchen and Mustards Grill in Napa Valley; author of *The Fog City Diner Cookbook* and the James Beard Foundation award–winning *Mustards Grill Napa Valley Cookbook*; and former executive chef/partner of several northern California restaurants, including Buckeye Roadhouse in Mill Valley, Miramonte and Tra Vigne in St. Helena, and Fog City Diner in San Francisco.

Caprial Pence (2002) Host of several PBS television cooking shows; chef/co-owner of Caprial's Bistro and cooking school in Portland, Oregon; author of *Caprial's Seasonal Kitchen* and five other cookbooks; and recipient of a James Beard Award for Best Chef: Pacific Northwest.

John Pence (2002) Cohost of *Caprial and John Cook for Friends* on PBS television and co-owner of Caprial's Bistro and cooking school in Portland, Oregon.

Jamie Purviance (2002) Author of *Weber's Art of the Grill* and *Weber's Big Book of Grilling*; editor of *The Barefoot Contessa Cookbook;* cooking teacher; former executive chef for St. Supéry Vineyards; and former food editor of *Appellation—Wine Country Living* magazine.

William Rice (1991) Principal food and wine columnist for the *Chicago Tribune*; author of *Feast of Wine and Food in America* and *Where to Eat in America*; former editor-in-chief of *Food & Wine* magazine; and former executive food editor of the *Washington Post*.

Judy Rodgers (1994) Chef/owner of Zuni Cafe in San Francisco; recipient of a James Beard Award for America's Outstanding Chef of the Year; author of *The Zuni Cafe Cookbook,* winner of the James Beard Award for Cookbook of the Year and an IACP award; and former chef of Union Hotel in Benicia, California, Chez Panisse in Berkeley, California, and Troisgros in Roanne, France.

Anne Rosenzweig (1993) Chef/co-owner of Arcadia and vice chairman of 21 Club in New York and author of *The Arcadia Seasonal Mural and Cookbook.*

Donna Scala (1999) Chef/co-owner of Bistro Don Giovanni in Napa, California; former chef/co-owner of Scala's Bistro in San Francisco; cocreator of Piatti Ristorante in Yountville, California; and former co-owner of Donarcy's gourmet food store in Sausalito, California.

Giovanni Scala (2001) Co-owner of Bistro Don Giovanni in Napa, California; former co-owner of Scala's Bistro in San Francisco; and cocreator of Piatti Ristorante in Yountville, California.

Chris Schlesinger (1990 and 1993) Chef/owner of East Coast Grill, Jake & Earl's Dixie Barbeque, and the Blue Room, all in Cambridge, Massachusetts; coauthor of numerous cookbooks with John Willoughby, including the James Beard Foundation award–winning *The Thrill of the Grill, Let the Flames Begin,* and *License to Grill*; and recipient of a James Beard Award for Best Chef: Northeast.

Arthur Schwartz (2000) Former host of daily *Arthur Schwartz with Food Talk* on WOR Radio in New York City; cooking teacher; and author of *Soup Suppers, What to Cook When You Think There's Nothing in the House to Eat, Cooking in a Small Kitchen,* and *Naples at Table*.

Susan Spungen (2003) Founding food editor of *Martha Stewart Living* magazine; former director of all things food for Martha Stewart Living Omnimedia; and coauthor of the IACP award–winning *Martha Stewart's Hors D'Oeuvres Handbook.*

Jeffrey Starr (1999 and 2000) Culinary director and chef of Sutter Home Winery; Napa Valley Mustard Festival "Chef of the Year"; culinary chair of the 2003 Napa Valley Wine Auction; opening chef of Crescent Club in Dallas, Texas, and Coyote Cafe in Santa Fe, New Mexico; former executive chef of Malibu Adobe in Malibu, California; and former owner of Starr Caterers in Napa Valley.

Harvey Steiman (1991) Editor-at-large of *Wine Spectator* magazine; host of *In the Kitchen with Harvey* radio show; and former food and wine editor of the *San Francisco Examiner*.

Zanne Stewart (1996) Food editor of *Gourmet* magazine and former board member and chair of the Julia Child Cookbook Awards for the IACP.

Steven Tevere (2001) Chef at Left Bank in San Mateo, California; former chef at Meadowood resort in St. Helena, California, Left Bank in Larkspur, California, and Boulevard in San Francisco.

Bob Trinchero (1990, 1991, 1994, 1996, and 1998) Chairman of the board and former chief executive officer of Trinchero Family Estates and Sutter Home Family Vineyards; member of the Napa Valley Vintner's Association and Napa Valley Wine Technical Group; named "Citizen of the Year" by the St. Helena Chamber of Commerce; recipient of the Distinguished Service Award by *Wine Spectator* magazine; and cochair of the 2003 Napa Valley Wine Auction.

Roger Trinchero (1993 and 1995) Vice chairman and chief executive officer and former president and chief operating officer of Trinchero Family Estates and Sutter Home Family Vineyards, and cochair of the 2003 Napa Valley Wine Auction.

Barbara Tropp (1993) Late chef/owner of China Moon Cafe in San Francisco; food product entrepreneur; cooking teacher; and author of *The Modern Art of Chinese Cooking, The China Diet,* and the IACP award–winning *China Moon Cookbook.*

Tina Ujlaki (2003) Executive food editor of *Food & Wine* magazine; former cookbook editor for Time-Life Books; and former translator of French cookbooks into English.

Patricia Unterman (1998) Chef/owner of Hayes Street Grill and Vicolo Pizzeria in San Francisco; author of *Food Lover's Guide to San Francisco* and the *Unterman on Food* newsletter; and restaurant reviewer and food writer for the *San Francisco Examiner.*

Jennifer Crutcher Wilkinson (1996) Food and entertaining editor of *Ladies' Home Journal* magazine; former food and entertaining editor of *Traditional Home* magazine; freelance food writer for the *Washington Post* and other newspapers and magazines; and former food editor for the *Northern Virginia Sun.*

John Willoughby (1990 and 1993) Executive editor of *Gourmet* magazine; coauthor of numerous cookbooks with Chris Schlesinger, including the James Beard Foundation award–winning *The Thrill of the Grill, Let the Flames Begin,* and *License to Grill*; contributor to numerous magazines and major metropolitan newspapers; and former senior editor of *Cook's Illustrated* magazine.

John Zehnder (2003) Executive chef and food and beverage director for Zehnder's of Frankenmuth in Michigan; regional vice president of American Culinary Federation; recipient of twenty-eight national awards for culinary competitions and recipe contests; author of two cookbooks about his restaurant; and consultant and recipe developer for commercial food products and marketing boards.

Judge

James McNair
St. Helena, California

Cook-Offs

All

**Chef Starr's
Wine Pairing**

Shiraz (Syrah)

Comments

"Given the chance to
enter the contest,
I might go with this
recipe, which teams
several American
favorite flavors to create
a new classic."

BBB (Barbecue, Bacon, & Blue) Burgers

Barbecue Glaze

1½ cups ketchup

½ cup firmly packed dark brown sugar

3 tablespoons apple cider vinegar

3 tablespoons Worcestershire sauce

2 tablespoons puréed canned chipotle chiles
  in adobo

1½ tablespoons yellow American mustard

Red Onion Mayonnaise

¾ cup mayonnaise

6 tablespoons finely chopped red onion

1½ tablespoons freshly squeezed lemon juice

12 thick bacon slices

Patties

2 pounds freshly ground pork

2 teaspoons salt

¾ teaspoon freshly ground black pepper

Vegetable oil, for brushing on the grill rack

6 cracked-wheat hamburger buns, split

8 ounces crumbled Maytag blue cheese

3 cups shredded crisp iceberg lettuce

18 bread-and-butter pickle slices

● Prepare a medium-hot fire in a charcoal grill with a cover, or preheat a gas grill to medium-high.

● To make the glaze, combine all of the ingredients in a small, heavy fire-proof saucepan. Place on the grill rack and cook, stirring frequently, until thickened slightly, about 10 minutes. Transfer about half of the sauce to a small bowl to use for drizzling on the finished burgers. Set the remainder aside in the pan for glazing the patties.

● To make the mayonnaise, combine all of the ingredients in a small bowl and mix well. Cover and refrigerate until serving.

● Place the bacon in a fire-proof skillet and cook on the grill rack, draining and discarding excess fat, until crisp. Transfer to paper towels to drain well. When cool enough to handle, crumble the bacon.

● To make the patties, combine the pork, salt, and pepper in a large bowl. Handling the meat as little as possible to avoid compacting it, mix well. Divide the mixture into 6 equal portions and form the portions into patties to fit the buns.

● When the grill is ready, brush the grill rack with vegetable oil. Place the patties on the rack and grill until browned on the bottoms, about 3 minutes. Turn the patties and brush the browned sides with the glaze. Continue grilling, turning and brushing frequently with the glaze, until done to preference, about 5 minutes longer for medium. During the last few minutes of cooking, place the buns, cut side down, on the outer edges of the rack to toast lightly. During the last minute of cooking, top each patty with an equal portion of the cheese to warm.

● To assemble the burgers, drizzle the reserved glaze on the bottom halves of the toasted buns and spread the toasted side of the bun tops with the mayonnaise. On each bun bottom, add ½ cup of the lettuce, a patty, an equal portion of the crumbled bacon, and 3 pickle slices. Add the bun tops and serve. *Makes 6 burgers*

Cuban-Style Burgers with Grilled Ham & Cheese

Mustard-Pickle Spread

¼ cup dill pickle relish

¼ cup yellow American mustard

¼ cup spicy brown mustard

Patties

1 pound freshly ground sirloin

1 teaspoon minced garlic

1 teaspoon chile powder

1 teaspoon ground cumin

2 tablespoons chopped cilantro

5 dashes TABASCO Pepper Sauce

Kosher salt

Freshly ground black pepper

Vegetable oil, for brushing on the grill rack

4 slices baked ham

4 thick slices Monterey Jack cheese

4 large sesame seed buns, split and brushed
   with butter

• Prepare a medium-hot fire in a charcoal grill with a cover, or preheat a gas grill to medium-high.

• To make the spread, combine the relish and mustards in a small bowl and stir to blend. Set aside.

• To make the patties, combine the sirloin, garlic, chile powder, cumin, cilantro, and pepper sauce in a large bowl and season with salt and pepper. Handling the meat as little as possible to avoid compacting it, mix well. Divide the mixture into 4 equal portions and form the portions into patties to fit the buns.

• When the grill is ready, brush the grill rack with vegetable oil. Place the patties on the rack, cover, and cook, turning once, until done to preference, 5 to 7 minutes on each side for medium. Just before the patties are done, turn a second time and place a ham slice and a cheese slice on top of each patty. During the last few minutes of cooking, place the buns, cut side down, on the outer edges of the rack to toast lightly.

• To assemble the burgers, spread the pickle spread over the cut sides of the buns. On each bun bottom, place a patty. Add the bun tops and serve. *Makes 4 burgers*

Judges
Chris Schlesinger,
Cambridge,
Massachusetts, and
John Willoughby,
New York, New York

Cook-Offs
1990 & 1993

Chef Starr's
Wine Pairing
Shiraz (Syrah)

Comments
"We both really enjoyed
judging the burger
contest. It is always
refreshing to share in the
joy of creativity and
accomplishment of
home cooks. They were
so proud and so happy.
It reminded Chris of
when he first started to
cook professionally."

Judges

Bob & Roger Trinchero,
Napa Valley, California

Cook-Offs

Bob—1990, 1991, 1994,
1996, & 1998
Roger—1993 & 1995

**Chef Starr's
Wine Pairing**

Zinfandel

Comments

"Along with our sister,
Vera, we grew up with
the flavors found in this
recipe—not surprising
with parents who were
great cooks. Our mother
kept a traditional Italian
kitchen that was reminis-
cent of our grandfather
Luigi's home in the small
seaport town of Savona,
north of Genoa."

Savona Burgers with Crispy Pancetta and Salsa Verde

Salsa Verde

1 bunch fresh flat-leaf parsley

1 bunch fresh mint

1 bunch fresh basil

¼ cup brine-packed capers, rinsed and drained

¼ cup chopped gherkins

3 white anchovy fillets, patted dry

2 garlic cloves

1 tablespoon Dijon mustard

1 tablespoon red wine vinegar

2 teaspoons sugar

2 teaspoons crushed red pepper flakes

½ cup olive oil

Salt

Freshly ground black pepper

Cheese Spread

½ cup shredded fresh mozzarella cheese (about 3 ounces)

¼ cup grated Parmesan cheese (about 1 ounce)

¼ cup crumbled Gorgonzola cheese (about 1 ounce)

2 green onions, minced

¼ cup mayonnaise

1 tablespoon chopped fresh garlic

1 teaspoon freshly ground black pepper

Patties

2 pounds ground chuck

Salt

Freshly ground black pepper

Vegetable oil, for brushing on the grill rack

4 focaccia buns, split

4 pancetta slices, cooked until crispy

4 vine-ripened beefsteak tomato slices

● Prepare a medium-hot fire in a charcoal grill with a cover, or preheat a gas grill to medium-high.

● To make the salsa, wash and thoroughly dry the herbs. Pick off the leaves and transfer them to a food processor. Add the capers, gherkins, anchovies, and garlic and process until finely chopped. Scrape the mixture into a bowl and stir in the mustard, vinegar, sugar, pepper flakes, and olive oil. Season to taste with salt and pepper. Cover and refrigerate.

● To make the spread, thoroughly mix the cheeses, green onions, mayonnaise, garlic, and pepper in a bowl. Cover and refrigerate.

● To make the patties, divide the beef into 4 equal portions and form the portions into patties to fit the buns. Season the patties with salt and pepper.

● When the grill is ready, brush the grill rack with vegetable oil. Place the patties on the rack, cover, and cook, turning once, until done to preference, 5 to 7 minutes on each side for medium. Meanwhile, preheat a broiler.

● Smear about 2 tablespoons of the spread on the cut sides of each bun. Place the buns, cheese side up, under the preheated broiler until the spread is bubbly and slightly golden, 2 to 3 minutes.

● To assemble the burgers, on each bun bottom, place a patty, a generous serving of the salsa, a pancetta slice, and a tomato slice. Add the bun tops and serve. *Makes 4 burgers*

Perfect California Hamburger

1 sturdy, fresh, tender hamburger bun

3 to 4 tablespoons mayonnaise

4 tablespoons finely chopped onion

Vegetable oil or shortening

¼ to ⅓ pound fresh ground beef with at least
    ⅓ part fat

Salt

Freshly ground black pepper

2 to 3 tablespoons sweet pickle relish

⅓ cup shaved (chiffonade) clean, crisp
    iceberg lettuce

Only if you must

2 tablespoons ballpark mustard (no Dijon)

2 tablespoons ketchup

Cheese (only mild Cheddar, please)

• Slice the hamburger bun in half. Stir the mayonnaise and onion together (so the onion doesn't slide around and become unevenly distributed) and spread on one half of the bun (a dry hamburger is not acceptable).

• Heat a skillet and lightly grease the bottom with a little oil or shortening. Lightly form the meat into a patty and put it into the hot skillet. Salt and pepper the top very liberally. Fry for 2 or 3 minutes (don't press down with a spatula because this will dry the meat). Turn the patty over and salt and pepper it again. Fry until cooked to your liking.

• Put the hamburger patty on the bun with the onion mayonnaise, and spread the other half of the bun with a liberal amount of relish and whatever additional condiments you may be using. Spread the lettuce over, add a slice of cheese, if you must, and put the bun together. *Makes 1 burger*

Adapted from *The Supper Book* by Marion Cunningham (Alfred A. Knopf, New York, 1992) and used by permission of the publisher.

Judge

Marion Cunningham,
Walnut Creek, California

Cook-Offs

1993, 1994, & 2000

**Chef Starr's
Wine Pairing**

White Zinfandel

Comments

"My hamburger creden-
tials come from the home
of the one and only
authentic hamburger,
which was developed in
Glendale, California, in
1936 by Bob Wian, the
man who turned one
rickety hamburger stand
into a chain of 1,136 Bob's
Big Boy restaurants.
In order to make this
hamburger, you cannot
allow yourself any
creative license."

Judge

Mark Miller
Santa Fe, New Mexico

Cook-Off

1994

**Chef Starr's
Wine Pairing**

Pinot Noir

Comments

"Caramelization of the
chiles is key to the
success of these burgers.
If you grind the meat and
know its lineage, the
burger can be eaten on
the rare side, but if you
buy the meat already
ground, cook to the
medium stage."

Quatro Chiles Secos (Four Dried Chiles) Burgers with Chipotle Chile Mayonnaise

Chipotle Chile Mayonnaise

1 cup mayonnaise

½ cup minced canned chipotle chiles in
   adobo sauce

1 tablespoon puréed roasted garlic

Juice of ½ lime

Patties

2 teaspoons plus 2 tablespoons corn oil

¼ cup minced white onion

¼ cup diced bacon

½ cup minced rehydrated dried guajillo chiles

½ cup puréed canned chipotle chiles in
   adobo sauce

2 teaspoons ground dried chile de árbol

2 teaspoons ground dried New Mexico red chile

2 teaspoons ground dried porcini mushrooms

2 teaspoons dried Mexican oregano

2 teaspoons salt

2 pounds ground chuck

¼ cup minced cilantro

4 Mexican bolillo buns or crusty sweet French rolls, split, fresh or toasted

12 avocado slices

4 large ripe tomato slices

4 red onion slices

● To make the mayonnaise, combine all of the ingredients in a small bowl and mix well. Cover and refrigerate until serving.

● To make the patties, heat an 8-inch sauté pan over a medium heat. Add 2 teaspoons of the corn oil, the onion, and the bacon and cook until the bacon is crisp. Add the 4 kinds of chiles, mushrooms, oregano, and salt. Cook over medium heat, stirring and scraping the pan to prevent scorching, for 5 minutes. Set aside to cool.

● Combine the beef, cilantro, and cooled chile mixture in a large bowl. Handling the meat as little as possible to avoid compacting it, mix well. Divide the mixture into 4 equal portions and form the portions into patties to fit the buns.

● Heat the remaining 2 tablespoons corn oil in a cast-iron skillet over medium heat. Add the patties and cook until done to preference, 5 to 7 minutes per side for medium. (There is a lot of liquid in the meat so be careful of splattering; you may wish to pour off some of the fat during cooking or cover with a splatter screen.)

● To assemble the burgers, spread the mayonnaise over the cut sides of the buns. On each bun bottom, place a patty, 3 avocado slices, a tomato slice, and an onion slice. Add the bun tops and serve. *Makes 4 burgers*

Mini Duck Burgers with Shiitake Mushroom Ketchup and Hot-Sweet Mustard Sauce

Hoisin Marinade

½ cup hoisin sauce

1 to 2 green onions, white and a bit of
the tender green, minced

2 tablespoons minced cilantro leaves and
tender stems

2¼ teaspoons minced garlic

2¼ teaspoons tamari

2¼ teaspoons sherry vinegar

2¼ teaspoons unseasoned rice vinegar

1½ teaspoons Asian sesame oil

1½ teaspoons sugar

¾ teaspoon Asian black bean–chile sauce or
chile-garlic sauce

¾ teaspoon peeled and grated fresh ginger

½ teaspoon TABASCO Pepper Sauce

¼ to ½ teaspoon freshly ground white pepper

Patties

2 pounds ground duck

2 green onions, white and a bit of the tender
green, minced

½ inch peeled and grated fresh ginger

1 tablespoon minced garlic

2 teaspoons salt

½ teaspoon freshly ground black pepper

Shiitake Mushroom Ketchup

2 to 3 tablespoons olive oil

1 pound shiitake mushrooms, stemmed
and quartered

1 onion, finely diced

¼ cup balsamic vinegar

¼ bunch chopped fresh basil

2 tablespoons molasses

2 teaspoons minced garlic

½ teaspoon salt

½ teaspoon freshly ground black pepper

Hot-Sweet Mustard Sauce

½ cup sugar

¼ cup Coleman's mustard powder

2 egg yolks

½ cup red wine vinegar

¾ cup crème fraîche or sour cream

Vegetable oil, for brushing on the grill rack

16 small sesame brioche buns, split

Butter, at room temperature, for spreading
on the buns

2 cups arugula

(continued)

Judge

Cindy Pawlcyn
St. Helena, California

Cook-Offs

1995 & 2000

**Chef Starr's
Wine Pairing**

Cabernet Sauvignon

Comments

"The duck can be
bought ground, or if
you prefer, you can
grind it at home. I use
almost 85 percent meat
to 15 percent fat/skin.
You should have pretty
good luck finding
sesame brioche buns at
a local bakery, but any
sesame seed bun you
like would work."

Mini Duck Burgers with Shiitake Mushroom Ketchup and Hot-Sweet Mustard Sauce (continued)

- To make the marinade, combine all of the ingredients in a stainless steel or ceramic bowl and whisk to blend well. Cover and refrigerate until needed.

- To make the patties, combine the duck, green onions, ginger, garlic, salt, pepper, and 2 tablespoons of the hoisin marinade in a large bowl. Handling the meat as little as possible to avoid compacting it, mix well. Cover and chill for at least 1 hour or up to overnight.

- To make the ketchup, heat the olive oil in a large sauté pan over medium-high heat. Add the mushrooms and cook until tender. Add the onion and cook until translucent. Add ¼ cup of the hoisin marinade, the vinegar, basil, molasses, garlic, salt, and pepper and stir to coat the mushrooms evenly. Decrease the heat and simmer until the liquid is thick enough to coat the mushrooms, 3 to 5 minutes. Cover and refrigerate until serving.

- To make the sauce, combine the sugar and mustard powder in the top of a double boiler and mix well with a whisk to prevent lumps. When well combined, whisk in the egg yolks and vinegar. Cook over simmering water, stirring occasionally, until it is thick enough to form ribbons when drizzled from a spoon, 10 to 15 minutes. Remove from the heat and allow the mixture to cool. When cool, fold in the crème fraîche. Cover and refrigerate until serving.

- Prepare a medium-hot fire in a charcoal grill with a cover, or preheat a gas grill to medium-high.

- When the grill is ready, brush the grill rack with vegetable oil. Divide the chilled patty mixture into 16 equal portions and form the portions into mini-patties to fit the buns. Place the patties on the rack and cover the grill. Cook, turning once and basting with some of the marinade, just until the juices run clear when the patties are pierced in the center, about 4 minutes on each side. During the last few minutes of cooking, place the buns, cut side down, on the outer edges of the rack to toast lightly.

- To assemble the burgers, spread softened butter on the cut sides of the buns. On each bun bottom, place a patty, mushroom ketchup to taste, a few arugula leaves, and a drizzle of the mustard sauce. Add the bun tops and serve with any extra ketchup and mustard sauce on the side. *Makes 16 mini-burgers*

Judges

Donna & Giovanni Scala
Napa, California

Cook-Offs

Donna—1999
Giovanni—2001

Chef Starr's
Wine Pairing

Zinfandel

Comments

"This simple burger
delights our regular
patrons, including
many Napa Valley
vintners and foodies."

Bistro Don Giovanni Burgers

Bistro Buns

1 cup plus 2 tablespoons milk

1 (0.6-ounce) cake compressed fresh yeast, or
    1 packet (2¼ teaspoons) active dry yeast

3 cups all-purpose flour

2 teaspoons kosher or sea salt

3 tablespoons olive oil

Olive oil, for brushing the bowl and the buns

Aioli

2 garlic cloves

1 teaspoon kosher or sea salt

1 egg yolk

1 cup extra virgin olive oil

Patties

3 pounds freshly ground chuck

3 teaspoons kosher or sea salt

2 teaspoons freshly ground black pepper

3 red onions, sliced thickly

Kosher or sea salt

Freshly ground black pepper

Olive oil, for drizzling on onions

Vegetable oil, for brushing on the grill rack

● To make the buns, warm the milk to body temperature and place in the bowl of a heavy-duty stand mixer fitted with a dough hook. Add the yeast and stir well to combine. Add the flour, salt, and 3 tablespoons olive oil. Mix on medium speed for 45 seconds. Brush a bowl generously with olive oil and, using a bowl scraper, transfer the very sticky dough to the oiled bowl. Cover the bowl with plastic wrap and set in a warm place until the dough is almost doubled in bulk, about 45 minutes if using fresh yeast, or about 1½ hours if using dry yeast.

● Line a baking sheet with kitchen parchment. Transfer the dough to a lightly floured work surface and sprinkle the dough surface lightly with flour. Divide the dough into 6 equal pieces. Dust your hands with flour and shape each piece of dough into a ball. Place the dough balls on the prepared baking sheet, brush each ball with olive oil, and let rest for 20 minutes.

● Preheat the oven to 375°F.

● Flatten each dough ball slightly into a bun shape. Bake until golden brown, about 25 minutes. Transfer to a wire rack to cool and brush the buns with a little more olive oil. When cool, slice horizontally in half.

● Prepare a medium-hot fire in a charcoal grill with a cover, or preheat a gas grill to medium-high.

● To make the aioli, smash the garlic and salt on a cutting board with the side of a large knife, or ideally in a mortar with a pestle, until you have a smooth paste. Transfer the paste to a mixing bowl. With a wire whisk, blend the egg yolk into the paste until smooth. While continuously whisking, slowly drizzle the olive oil into the bowl. The sauce will be tight, intensely garlicky, and sticky when finished. If you wish a lighter sauce, whisk in a little water to loosen it up.

● To make the patties, spread the beef out in a shallow pan. Sprinkle evenly with the salt and pepper. Handling the meat as little as possible to avoid compacting it, mix well. Divide the mixture into 6 equal portions and form the portions into patties to fit the buns.

(continued)

Bistro Don Giovanni Burgers (continued)

- Sprinkle the onion slices to taste with salt and pepper and drizzle with olive oil.

- When the grill is ready, brush the grill rack with vegetable oil. Place the patties on the rack, cover, and cook, turning once, until done to preference, 5 to 7 minutes on each side for medium. Place the onion slices on the rack and grill until caramelized and tender, 10 to 15 minutes. During the last few minutes of cooking, place the buns, cut side down, on the outer edges of the rack to toast lightly.

- To assemble the burgers, smother the cut side of the bun tops with aioli. On each bun bottom, place a patty and an equal portion of the grilled onions. Add the bun tops and serve.

Makes 6 burgers

Kobe Patty Melts with Fresh Pickles and Peppadew Mayonnaise

Fresh Pickles

1 English cucumber, halved lengthwise,
 seeded, and sliced diagonally 1/8 inch thick

2 tablespoons thinly sliced red onion

2 tablespoons thinly sliced red bell pepper

1/2 cup Champagne vinegar

1/4 cup sugar

1 1/2 teaspoons pink peppercorns

1 1/2 teaspoons yellow mustard seed

1/2 teaspoon coriander seed

Salt

Peppadew Mayonnaise

1 cup bottled South African Peppadew
 peppers, drained

3/4 cup Best Foods or Hellmann's mayonnaise

Caramelized Onions

3 tablespoons olive oil

2 yellow onions, peeled, halved, and sliced
 1/4 inch thick

Salt

Freshly ground black pepper

Patties

2 pounds ground American Kobe beef

Salt

Freshly ground black pepper

8 extra-sour rye bread slices

4 tablespoons butter, melted

1/2 pound Vermont Cheddar cheese, shredded

● To make the pickles, combine the cucumber, onion, and bell pepper in a heat-proof bowl and set aside. Combine the vinegar, sugar, peppercorns, mustard seed, and coriander seed in a small saucepan and place over medium heat. Bring the vinegar mixture to a simmer, and then adjust the heat to maintain a simmer and cook for 5 minutes. Pour the vinegar mixture over the vegetables in the bowl and season to taste with salt. Cover and refrigerate overnight, stirring occasionally.

● To make the mayonnaise, combine the peppers with the mayonnaise in a blender or food processor and process until smooth. (Optionally, pass the mixture through a fine-mesh strainer and transfer to a squirt bottle.) Cover and refrigerate.

● To make the onions, heat the olive oil in a large sauté pan over medium-low heat. Add the onions, sprinkle with salt, and cook, stirring frequently, for 15 minutes. Increase the heat to medium and continue cooking until the onions are caramelized and golden brown, about 15 minutes longer. Season to taste with salt and pepper and set aside.

● To make the patties, season the beef with salt and pepper in a large bowl. Handling the meat as little as possible to avoid compacting it, mix well. Divide the mixture into 4 equal

(continued)

Judge

Jeffrey Starr
St. Helena, California

Cook-Offs

1999 & 2000

**Chef Starr's
Wine Pairing**

Pinot Noir

Comments

"As a kid, my favorite
hamburger in the world
was a patty melt. This is
a sophisticated version,
using ultra-tender
American Kobe beef.
If you can't find it, substitute top-quality ground
chuck. For a crisp and
cool contrast, I add
mayonnaise and pickles
to the cooked patties."

Kobe Patty Melts with Fresh Pickles and Peppadew Mayonnaise (continued)

portions and form the portions into patties to fit the bread slices. Heat a cast-iron skillet over medium-high heat and cook the patties, turning once, until done to your liking, 5 to 7 minutes on each side for medium.

- Brush 1 side of each bread slice with melted butter. Place 4 bread slices, buttered side down, on a cutting board. Sprinkle half of the cheese over the 4 slices, dividing equally. Top the cheese on each slice with an equal portion of the onions, a cooked patty, and then an equal portion of the remaining cheese. Top with the remaining 4 bread slices, buttered side up.

- Heat a large nonstick skillet over medium heat. Place the patty melts in the skillet and cook until the bottoms are golden brown. Turn and cook the other sides until golden. Remove from the skillet and carefully lift off the top slices of bread. Generously spread or drizzle the mayonnaise over each beef patty and top each patty with 3 tablespoons or more to taste of the pickles. Re-cover the patties with the top bread slices, cut each patty melt in half, and serve. *Makes 4 burgers*

Judge
Bruce Aidells
Kensington, California

Cook-Off
2000

**Chef Starr's
Wine Pairing**
Pinot Noir

Comments
"Stuffing the patties
with cheese helps keep
the patties moist and
provides a pleasant
surprise. Allow guests
to add ketchup and/or
other condiments, such
as raw onion or sliced
pickles, if desired."

Pork Burgers Stuffed with Mozzarella Cheese

Roasted Mushrooms

¼ cup olive oil

1 teaspoon minced garlic

4 large portobello mushrooms, stems removed

Salt

Freshly ground black pepper

Lemon-Sage Mayonnaise

½ cup mayonnaise

1 teaspoon grated lemon zest

½ teaspoon dried sage

2 teaspoons whole-grain mustard

Patties

1½ pounds ground pork

1 teaspoon minced garlic

2 teaspoons Worcestershire sauce

1 teaspoon salt

¾ teaspoon freshly ground black pepper

1 cup shredded mozzarella cheese
(about 3 ounces)

¼ cup finely chopped green onions

1 tablespoon olive oil

4 large sesame buns, split, fresh or toasted

- Preheat the oven to 400°F.

- To make the mushrooms, combine the olive oil and garlic in a small bowl and brush the mixture generously on both the gill and top sides of the mushrooms. Sprinkle both sides of the mushrooms to taste with salt and pepper. Place the mushrooms, gill side down, on a baking sheet and roast in the oven for 10 minutes. Turn the mushrooms over and continue roasting until tender, 5 to 10 minutes longer. Set aside.

- To make the mayonnaise, combine all of the ingredients in a small bowl and mix well. Cover and refrigerate until serving.

- To make the patties, combine the pork, garlic, Worcestershire sauce, salt, and pepper in a large bowl. Handling the meat as little as possible to avoid compacting it, mix well. Divide the mixture into 8 equal portions and form the portions into patties to fit the buns. Combine the cheese and onions in a bowl and mix well. Place equal amounts of the cheese mixture on the center of 4 of the patties. Cover the filling with the remaining 4 patties and press all around to seal the edges.

- Heat the olive oil in a 12-inch skillet over medium-high heat. Add the patties and cook, turning once, until done to preference, about 5 minutes on each side for medium-well.

- To assemble the burgers, spread the mayonnaise over the cut sides of the buns. On each bun bottom, place a patty and a mushroom. Add the bun tops and serve. *Makes 4 burgers*

Curry Chicken Burgers with Carrot Salad

Carrot Salad

3 tablespoons olive oil

1½ tablespoons freshly squeezed lemon juice

1 teaspoon Dijon mustard

½ teaspoon sugar

Salt

Freshly ground black pepper

3 cups peeled and grated carrots

1 tablespoon snipped fresh chives

Patties

2 tablespoons olive oil

½ cup diced (¼ inch) red onion

2 teaspoons curry powder

1 pound ground chicken or turkey

1 small egg, lightly beaten

½ cup fresh bread crumbs

¼ cup peeled and grated Granny Smith apple

¼ cup chopped mango chutney

2 green onions, including green tops, thinly
    sliced on the diagonal

Salt

Freshly ground black pepper

Vegetable oil, for brushing on the grill rack

4 hamburger buns, split

Mayonnaise

• To make the salad, combine the olive oil, lemon juice, mustard, sugar, and salt and pepper to taste in a large bowl and whisk to mix well. Add the grated carrots and chives and toss with the dressing. Cover and refrigerate until serving.

• To make the patties, heat the olive oil in a nonstick skillet over medium-low heat. Add the onion and cook, stirring frequently, until soft and lightly browned, about 10 minutes. Decrease the heat to low, add the curry power, and cook, stirring constantly, for 1 minute to mellow the flavors. Transfer to a large bowl and set aside to cool.

• Add the chicken, egg, bread crumbs, apple, chutney, and green onions to the cooled onion mixture and season with salt and pepper. Handling the meat as little as possible to avoid compacting it, mix well. Divide the mixture into 4 equal portions and form the portions into patties to fit the buns. (At this point, you may wish to chill the patties for an hour or so before cooking for easier handling on the grill.)

• Prepare a medium-hot fire in a charcoal grill with a cover, or preheat a gas grill to medium-high.

• When the grill is ready, brush the grill rack with vegetable oil. Place the patties on the rack, cover, and cook, turning once, just until the juices run clear when the patties are pierced in the center, about 4 minutes on each side. During the last few minutes of cooking, place the buns, cut side down, on the outer edges of the rack to toast lightly.

• To assemble the burgers, spread mayonnaise to taste over the cut sides of the buns. On each bun bottom, place a patty and 2 tablespoons of the salad. Add the bun tops and serve. Pass the remaining salad. *Makes 4 burgers*

Judge

Sheila Lukins
New York, New York

Cook-Off

2000

**Chef Starr's
Wine Pairing**

Pinot Grigio

Comments

"Spending the weekend
at Sutter Home was a
great treat in itself, but
tasting so many original
and delicious burgers
was the icing on the cake.
The congeniality made
me want to return year
after year."

Judge

Arthur Schwartz
Brooklyn, New York

Cook-Off

2000

Chef Starr's Wine Pairing

Cabernet Sauvignon

Comments

"My idea of burger heaven is a thick, well-crusted but medium-rare disk of pure, freshly ground beef with enough fat and juiciness that it will drip down my chin should I eat it with abandon. It must be on a traditional soft bun—basically something to hold it with—and with ketchup."

Pure Beef Burgers

Smothered Onions (optional)

3 tablespoons butter

2 onions, sliced

Patties

1 pound freshly ground beef, such as a
combination of neck and hanger steak,
porterhouse tails, or ground chuck
(not too lean), well chilled

Medium-grain sea salt

2 thick extra-sharp Cheddar cheese
slices (optional)

2 white-bread buns (not crusty, dense, or
supposedly "better quality"), split, fresh
or toasted

Ketchup

- If you choose to serve the burgers with the onions, heat the butter in a skillet over medium heat until sizzling. Add the onions and sauté until well wilted, about 5 minutes. Decrease the heat to low and cook the onions about 20 minutes longer, stirring only occasionally, until the onions are soft and lightly browned. Set aside.

- Take half of the meat in your hands and shape it into a thick disk without compacting the meat much. Simply press it down lightly to flatten it, then rotate the disk in your hands, patting the edges smooth as you rotate to make a patty. The patty should be about the same diameter as the bun, so after it has shrunk in cooking it will be slightly smaller. Repeat with the remaining meat. Liberally salt the surface of the patties.

- To cook on top of the stove, heat a black iron skillet over high heat until very hot—a drop of water should evaporate instantly. Place the patties in the pan and, without moving them, flipping them, or squeezing them down, cook for 5 minutes. Turn the patties and cook another 4 to 6 minutes, depending on how done you like them. The shorter time will produce a rare burger, the longer time a medium burger.

- To cook the patties in the broiler, heat the broiler with the broiler pan in place (to preheat it) so that the burgers will be no more than 2 to 3 inches from the heat. Place the patties on the preheated broiler pan and broil for 5 minutes. Turn and broil until done to taste—another 4 to 6 minutes.

- For cheeseburgers, top each cooked patty with a slice of the cheese.

- To assemble the burgers, on each bun bottom, place a patty, a generous portion of ketchup, and an equal portion of the smothered onions (if using). Add the bun tops and serve. *Makes 2 burgers*

Grilled Feta Burgers with Wilted Spinach and Tomato-Stewed Onions and Olives

Patties

4 whole garlic cloves (not peeled)

1¼ pounds ground chuck

½ cup crumbled feta cheese

¾ teaspoon dried oregano

½ teaspoon salt

½ teaspoon freshly ground black pepper

Tomato-Stewed Onions and Olives

2 tablespoons olive oil

1 very large onion, halved and sliced thinly
    (about 4 cups)

Salt

Freshly ground black pepper

½ cup petite diced tomatoes
    (from a 14½-ounce can)

¼ cup pitted Kalamata olives,
    chopped coarsely

Vegetable oil, for brushing on the grill rack

8 (4-inch) pita breads

Wilted Spinach

1 tablespoon olive oil

2 cloves garlic, minced

1 (9-ounce) bag prewashed spinach

Salt

Freshly ground black pepper

● To make the patties, put the whole garlic cloves in a small skillet over medium-high heat and toast until spotty brown on all sides, about 5 minutes. Remove from the skillet, peel, mince, and set aside.

● Break up the chuck in a large bowl. Sprinkle the skillet-toasted garlic, feta, oregano, salt, and pepper over the meat. Handling the meat as little as possible to avoid compacting it, mix well. Divide the mixture into 4 equal portions and form the portions into patties to fit the pita breads. Refrigerate until ready to cook.

● To make the onions and olives, heat the olive oil in a large (12-inch) skillet over medium-high heat. Add the onions and sauté, seasoning to taste with salt and pepper, until golden brown, 8 to 10 minutes. Add the tomatoes and olives and cook until the tomato liquid evaporates, less than a minute. Transfer the mixture to a microwave-safe container and set aside. Do not wash the skillet.

● Prepare a medium-hot fire in a charcoal grill with a cover, or preheat a gas grill to medium-high.

● When the grill is ready, brush the grill rack with vegetable oil. Place the patties on the rack, cover, and cook, turning once, until done to preference, 5 to 7 minutes on each side for medium. During the last few minutes of cooking, place the pita breads on the outer edges of the rack to toast lightly. Remove the patties and breads from the grill and let rest for a few minutes while preparing the spinach and warming the onion mixture.

● To make the spinach, add the olive oil and garlic to the reserved skillet. Place over medium-high heat. When the garlic starts to sizzle and turn golden, add the spinach and sauté until just wilted, 1 to 2 minutes. Season to taste with salt and pepper.

● Warm the onions and olives in a microwave oven.

● To assemble the burgers, place a patty on 4 of the pita breads. Top each patty with an equal portion of the onions and olives and an equal portion of the spinach. Top with the remaining breads and serve. *Makes 4 burgers*

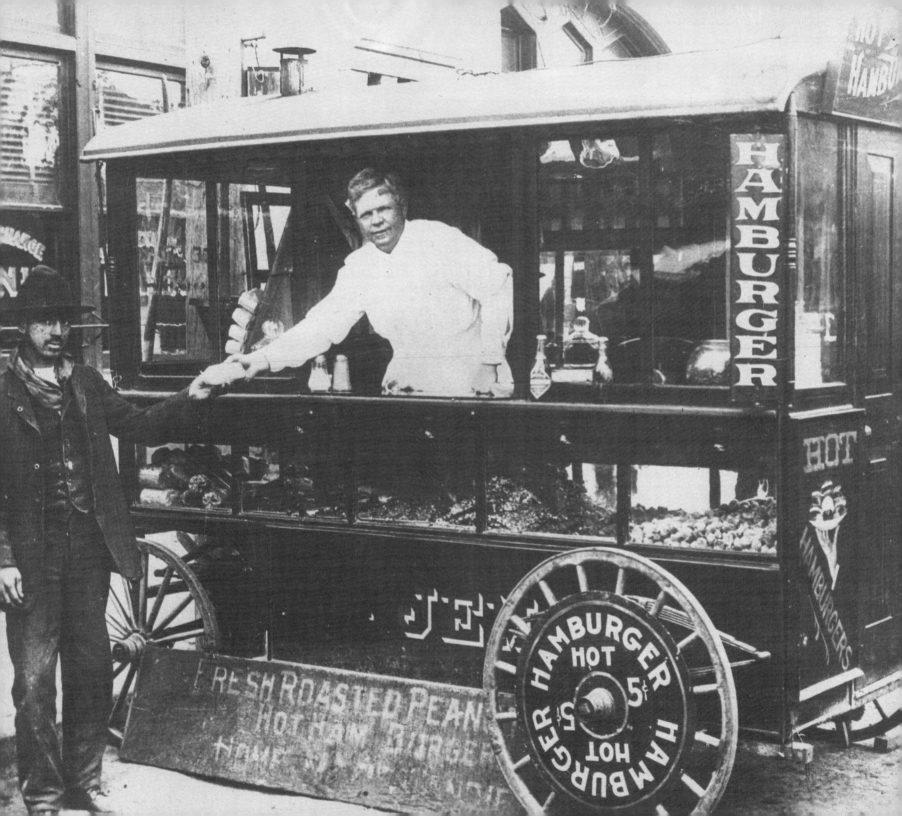

guidelines for success

Building a Burger

he latest rules of the Build a Better Burger recipe contest identify a burger as a grilled ground patty formed from any food product and served on a bun or other bread product, and it may include any combination of condiments, spreads, sauces, seasonings, cheeses, and toppings. Side dishes and garnishes to the plate are not allowed in the contest, so all ingredients included in a recipe must be assembled between the bread used to build the burger.

Although many people commonly refer to ground beef as "burger" or "hamburger," or to the patty as a "burger," the sandwich is not technically a "burger" until all of the components are put together. Here's the terminology favored by Build a Better Burger.

• Bun or other bread product, such as croissants, focaccia, sliced French bread, pita breads, or tortillas, must be used to hold the patty.

• Patty formed from any ground food product, including beans, beef, chicken, duck, lamb, pork, turkey, or tofu, must be grilled on a standard outdoor kettle-type grill.

• Cheese options include American, blue, feta, Cheddar, goat cheese, or any other favorite.

• Condiments can include barbecue sauce, chutney, ketchup, mayonnaise, mustard, salsa, tapenade, or other flavorful additions spread on the buns.

• Toppings placed on or under the patty can include lettuce or other greens, tomato slices, onion slices, pickles, grilled vegetables, or other similar ingredients.

Building Better Burgers

ecause any ground meat dries out quickly, purchase boneless meat and grind or mince it just before cooking, or buy freshly ground meat from a reliable butcher. To incorporate flavor into every bite, thoroughly mix seasonings into ground ingredients. Contrary to popular culinary myth, salting ground meat a few minutes before cooking will not draw out the moisture and create a dry burger. For our tastes, one teaspoon of salt to every pound of meat is a perfect ratio.

• If making beef burgers, keep in mind that the lower the fat content, the less flavor and the tougher the cooked patty. Ground chuck, usually around 24 percent fat, or other fatty cuts make the best patties.

• When using lean meats, add a little ground fat, a bit of wine or broth, and extra seasonings to keep the patties moist and flavorful.

• For a lighter texture and tender patties, handle the mixture as little as possible when mixing in seasonings and forming the patties to prevent compacting.

• Cook the patties shortly before serving.

• Brush the hot grill rack with vegetable oil before adding the patties to help keep them from sticking.

• Place the patties directly over the heat source if you want them well charred on the outside and moist and juicy inside.

- When grilling patties with a high fat content or dripping marinades, offset them from the fire to prevent flare-ups.

- To keep all of the delicious juices inside, avoid pressing down on the patties with a spatula during cooking.

- Many of us prefer our burger patties cooked less done, but for optimal safety the USDA recommends cooking beef, buffalo, lamb, pork, and veal patties to an internal temperature of 160°F and poultry patties to 165°F. It is recommended that fish patties be cooked until opaque throughout. To check the internal temperature, insert an instant-read thermometer into the center of a patty. If it is not thick enough to check from the top, the thermometer may be inserted from the side of the patty. Be sure to wash the thermometer after each trial.

- When topping with cheese, wait until the patties are almost done, then close the grill lid for quicker melting.

- Burgers taste best when the buns are warm and lightly toasted.

- Serve assembled burgers immediately.

Creating Winning Recipes

Here are some tips that may increase your chances of being selected as a BBB finalist, and many should also prove helpful in entering other recipe contests:

• Read the rules very carefully before working on a recipe. Rules are available shortly before Memorial Day each year at www.buildabetterburger.com or by mail from Sutter Home Family Vineyards, P.O. Box 248, St. Helena, CA 94574.

• Check recipes that have won the contest in previous years in this book or on the Build a Better Burger website. They are examples of how to write winning recipes and will also show you what has already been done and shouldn't be repeated.

• Stay up to date. Read food magazines, newspaper food sections, and the latest cookbooks, and watch cooking shows on television to keep up with what's going on in the world of food.

• Be creative and "think outside of the box." Keep in mind, however, that "original" does not equal weird, so make certain that the flavors of the ingredients all work together. Avoid being too trendy just for the sake of being different. Creative uses of traditional burger ingredients often work best.

• Choose a good name. "Aunt Betty's Burgers" or "Daddy's Favorite Burgers" aren't going to get a second look, but "Black Thai Burgers" or "My Big Fat Greek Burgers" will definitely grab attention. Descriptive straightforward names such as "Cajun Andouille and Shrimp Burgers with Fiery Tasso Mayonnaise" or "Caesar Salad and Flank Steak Burgers with Garlic Crostini" will also get noticed.

• List ingredients in the same order that they are used. This one requirement lands more recipes in the disqualified pile than anything else.

• Include every detail of building the burger in step-by-step directions and double-check that you mention the ingredients in the exact same order that they are given in the ingredients list. If you list "6 sesame hamburger buns" followed by "1/4 cup softened butter" in the ingredients list, direct people to "Spread the buns with the butter." Don't say, "Butter the buns," which is out of order and disqualifies a recipe.

• Don't make a screener or judge count when reading directions by having them combine "the first 6 ingredients" or "the next 14 ingredients," but call for each ingredient. If you do choose to use this style, remember that "salt and pepper" listed on one line in the ingredients list are two ingredients, not one.

• Don't end by saying, "Serve burgers with condiments of choice and/or on bun of choice." This is your recipe and should be submitted exactly as you want it and would prepare it at the cook-off, so specify the exact buns and condiments to use. And don't forget to specify amounts of each in the ingredients list.

• Use enough seasoning. Salt enhances flavor, so no matter how creative and interesting they sound, recipes that don't add enough salt to the patties won't make my first cut. BBB is judged by food professionals, including a lot of chefs, who are looking for the tastiest burger. The most frequent complaint from the judges is that the patties are underseasoned.

• Use fresh ingredients whenever possible. I'm more inclined to consider recipes that call for fresh garlic instead of garlic powder or fresh herbs instead of dried.

•Toast or heat the bread. In the final round of selections, unless everything else is superior to the other recipes that I'm considering, I cast aside those that assemble the burgers on cold buns.

•The use of Sutter Home wine and other sponsors' ingredients does not sway me in choosing the best recipes. On the other hand, these are the folks putting up the prize money, so it's nice to include their ingredients when appropriate. I definitely rule out a recipe that calls for wine produced by another winery or for a variety of wine that Sutter Home doesn't make, as that shows that you haven't done your homework for the contest.

• Before submitting your recipe, either electronically or by mail, be sure that you have followed the rules exactly. Reread the rules several times and double-check your written entry against them. For mailed entries, be sure to use the correct size of paper (BBB accepts only 8½ by 11-inch sheets), staple pages together when more than one page is used, and be sure to put your name and contact information at the top of the page. For all submissions, be sure that your contact information is complete and correct.

If you're selected as a finalist, here are a few tips that may boost your chances of winning the top prize:

• No matter how great the recipe, on cook-off day it all comes down to how well you can cook under pressure. Increase your odds of receiving that big check and chubby trophy with the same answer to the old joke about how to get to Carnegie Hall—Practice! Practice! Practice! Invite your family and friends and stage your own cook-off "rehearsals" at home to prepare for your "performance for the critics" in California. Remember that it's too late to make any changes to the submitted recipe, but you can perfect your cooking techniques.

• Good recipes have been done in at the cook-off because the finalists hadn't actually cooked their submissions on a charcoal grill before. The 2003 Grand Prize winner didn't have a charcoal grill on the balcony of her high-rise co-op in Jackson Heights, New York, so she made several trips to the home of friends with a grill to prepare her recipe before heading to Napa Valley.

• At the contestants' meeting on the afternoon before the cook-off, check the ingredients and equipment carefully to make certain that everything meets your expectations. As soon as you arrive at the cook-off, recheck the ingredients and equipment before starting to cook.

• Stay calm and focused. Don't be distracted by other contestants, visitors watching you from behind the ropes, television cameras, reporters, or photographers.

•Watch the clock. Have a game plan for completing everything on time, and stick to it.

• Keep a positive attitude. This is a cook-off where the judges can see you working and interacting with your fellow contestants, so don't turn us off before we even get a chance to taste your creation.

Pairing Wine with Burgers

The Culinary Director and Executive Chef for Sutter Home Family Vineyards, Jeffrey Starr creates foods to pair with Sutter Home wines for events at the winery. Guests often take a seat at the Chef's Table in the winery's Culinary Center, a state-of-the-art professional kitchen, where they can observe Jeffrey and his staff in action. The busy chef was named Napa Valley Mustard Festival's "Chef of the Year" in 2000 and 2001, and served as Culinary Chair of the famed Napa Valley Wine Auction in 2003.

Jeffrey is responsible for assembling the ingredients for the finalists in the Build a Better Burger cook-off and the finalists are treated to a special dinner created by the chef on the night before the competition. His idea for a perfect burger can be found on page 168.

As a winery chef, I focus on how well the food pairs with wine.

Pairing wine with French, Italian, and other European cuisines that have centuries-old wine traditions is generally fairly simple. They have developed dishes that go well with their local wines, and they grow grapes to vinify into wines that complement their food. In addition, these cuisines are generally wine-friendly because they lack chiles and other assertive flavors that can conflict with the wine.

Asian, Latin, and other global cuisines can be difficult to pair with wine. Those areas don't have a history of wine production and their cuisines have assertive flavors and can be very spicy. More often than not, we think of serving those foods with beer.

We often associate wine with "gourmet" food and special occasions. This snob appeal can be very intimidating for most people. We usually overlook simple, everyday dishes like the hamburger and relegate them to bubbly beverages like soda and beer. To me, pairing global cuisines and simple everyday foods with wine is fun.

The great thing about burgers is that you can create so many flavor combinations. And with the popularity of alternative cuisines, you see more of these flavors used in burgers. For me, wine, when properly paired with burgers, is more enjoyable than other beverages because it enhances the flavors of the burgers. A wonderful wine can really bring out the best in a burger, but don't feel that you have to pick just the right wine to pair with your burger creation. Chances are, if you like a particular wine, it will pair nicely with your burger. Just start experimenting with different combinations and find what you like. If it tastes good to you, it's a good food-and-wine pairing.

When I pair wine with food, I like to look at the "taste balance" between them. If the burger I create is properly balanced, it will come into balance with the wine. Put another way, anything you eat or drink will change the taste of the next thing you eat or drink. I don't want the food to negatively change the taste of the wine. I want the food to enhance the wine and the wine to enhance the food. A great food-and-wine pairing increases the enjoyment of both.

Have you ever brushed your teeth in the morning and then drunk a glass of orange juice? Yuck! Not a good pairing. The sweet toothpaste changes the taste of the orange juice, which becomes sour and bitter. It is this sort of taste reaction I address when pairing food with wine.

So how do we bring food and wine into "taste balance"? First, like orange juice, wine is acidic. So if we pair wine with sweet foods, the acidity in the wine can become very strong, just like sweet toothpaste enhances the acidity of orange juice. On the other hand, *because* wine is acidic, acidity in *food* will make the wine taste *milder.* The good news is that most burger condiments are sweet *and* sour (think ketchup and relish) and the balance between those two tastes will not adversely affect many wines. Many Asian and Pacific Rim dishes have similar sweet and sour tastes, so creating a burger using these flavors can be wonderful as long as you balance the sweet with the sour.

Asian, Latin, Moroccan, and other global dishes can often also be hot and spicy. The heat from chiles can make wines taste strong. That's why we avoid pairing the stronger, bigger, bolder wines like Cabernet Sauvignon with fiery dishes. Milder wines, such as Sauvignon Blanc, work better, and wines with a little sweetness, like White Zinfandel, better yet! The sweetness of the wine will help tame the fire of the chiles.

Here are some of my favorite pairings of Sutter Home wines with prize-winning burgers in this book:

Cabernet Sauvignon with Buttered Pecan Buffalo Burgers with Cabernet Cranberries and Herbed Mayonnaise (page 135). It sure helps pairing a dish with wine when you use that wine in the recipe! Buffalo is big and bold and you need a wine like Cabernet Sauvignon to stand up to it, and the Cabernet-soaked cranberries do a terrific job of bringing out the juicy cherry notes in the wine.

Chardonnay with Choucroute Burgers with Green Apple Salsa (page 49). The green apple salsa beautifully mirrors the apple notes of Chardonnay. The wine is crisp and light—perfect for the spicy, rich Italian-sausage-and-turkey burgers.

Chenin Blanc with Green Chile Chicken Burgers with Orange-Chili Mayonnaise and Three-Pepper Cheese Spread (page 73). Chenin Blanc is a wonderful picnic wine and I often serve it with cheese and fruit. And because it is off-dry, it also pairs nicely with mildly spicy food. This burger has all of these elements—orange, goat cheese, and chiles. So pour yourself a glass of Chenin Blanc when you make this burger.

Gewürztraminer with Beijing Burgers (page 53). When I think ginger, I think Gewürztraminer. The Chinese five-spice powder, ginger, rice vinegar, sesame, and soy of this burger have a magical marriage with the spicy, floral exotic fruit of this wine.

Merlot with Peppered Lamb Burgers with "Hot Tomato" Jam (page 60). Merlot with tomatoes and Merlot with lamb are classic combinations. The juicy, black cherry fruit of this wine perfectly complements the richness of this burger.

Pinot Grigio with Three-Nut Turkey Burgers with Tropical Fruit Salsa (page 41). The citrusy, tropical fruit of Pinot Grigio pairs nicely with the tropical fruit salsa. And the lighter flavors won't overwhelm the mild turkey-nut burger.

Pinot Noir with Portobello Burgers (page 59). Mushrooms and Pinot Noir are a natural. That earthy quality is carried through in both. And I especially like the way the herbal quality of the wine is mirrored in these very herbaceous burgers.

Sauvignon Blanc with Fresh Salmon Burgers with Lemon-Cilantro Mayonnaise (page 82). The crisp, bright, citrus fruit of the Sauvignon Blanc nicely mirrors the lemon in this recipe and provides a clean contrast to the rich salmon burger.

Shiraz with Chipotle-Honey BBQ Bacon Burgers with Gorgonzola Cheese (page 127). I'm often inclined to pair Shiraz with peppery, bacony, smoky foods because those qualities are found in the wine. This medium-bodied red varietal pairs nicely with the beef and pork in this burger, and the peppered bacon and smoky chipotle send the pairing over the top!

White Cabernet with Calypso Burgers (page 38). The crisp acidity of White Cabernet goes well with the hot pork sausage in these rich, spicy burgers. And the sweet fruit with blackberry nuances of the wine will cool off your mouth.

White Merlot with Spicy Summer Shrimp Burgers with Crisp Pancetta (page 124). This burger is filled with the taste of summer. It reminds me of a picnic at the beach, so enjoy it with the juicy, crisp raspberry flavors of this perfect picnic wine.

White Zinfandel with Chicken Oriental Burgers with Grilled Shiitake (page 69). White Zinfandel is a natural with mildly spicy Asian and Latin cuisines. The sweetness of the wine is nice with the spice of the burger, and it's mild enough to not compete with the delicate chicken.

Zinfandel with Italian Burgers with Confetti Salsa (page 37). When you think Italian, think Zinfandel! This spicy black-pepper, fruity wine is a great complement to the garlic, tomato, onion, olives, parsley, basil, and hot Italian sausage in these burger patties and to the mildly spicy salsa served on them.

Jim Pleasants,
Grand Prize 1990

Robert Chirico,
Grand Prize 1991

Robert Allen,
Grand Prize 1993
(not pictured)

Kurt Wait,
Grand Prize 1994

Porter Lansing,
Grand Prize 1995

Lori Welander,
Grand Prize 1996

Susan Asanovic,
Grand Prize 1997

Larry Elder,
Grand Prize 1998

Julie DeMatteo,
Grand Prize 1999

Annelle Williams,
Grand Prize 2002

Susan Mello,
Grand Prize 2003

Clint Stephenson,
Grand Prize 2004

Jamie Miller,
Grand Prize 2000

Kristine Snyder,
Grand Prize 2001

winners
& finalists

1990

Winners

Grand Prize: Jim Pleasants, Williamsburg, Virginia—Napa Valley Basil-Smoked Burgers

Second Prize: Betty Shenberger, Beaverton, Oregon—Mustard-Grilled Lamb Burgers with Grilled Eggplant Salsa

Third Prize: Priscilla Yee, Concord, California—Spicy Sausage Burgers with Roasted Pepper Relish

Award for Creativity: Wayne Fairchild, Shreveport, Louisiana—Hearty Southern Bean Burgers

Other Finalists*

A. Y. Atoulikian, Ohio

Rosemarie Berger, North Carolina

Betty Brown, Arizona

Mary Cummings, Massachusetts

Robert Cummisford, Wisconsin

Alex DeSantis, New Jersey

John Douglas, New Mexico

Lois Dowling, Tacoma, Washington—Oslo Burgers

Connie Emerson, Reno, Nevada—Foxy Loxy Burgers

Lee Jorik, Illinois

Mary Louise Lever, Rome, Georgia

Jacquelyn Paine, Baltimore, Maryland

Marina Polvay, Florida

Debbie Russell, Colorado Springs, Colorado

Linda Sarkisian, South Carolina

Angela Trusty, Indiana

*For many of the 1990 finalists, only the names and states in which they lived remain in Sutter Home's files. For the record, if you know the hometowns or the name of the burgers missing here, please contact BBB, Sutter Home Family Vineyards, P.O. Box 248, St. Helena, CA 94574.

1991

Winners

Grand Prize: Robert Chirico, Greenfield, Massachusetts—Lamburgers à la Grecque with Cilantro-Mint Chutney

First Prize: Debbie Russell, Colorado Springs, Colorado—Hazelnut-Crusted Lamb Burgers

Second Prize: Caryl Welsh, Clarksville, Maryland—Italian Burgers with Confetti Salsa

Third Prize: Dr. Helen Conwell, Fairhope, Alabama—Calypso Burgers

Award for Creativity: Theodore Skiba, Tequesta, Florida—Three-Nut Turkey Burgers with Tropical Fruit Salsa

Other Finalists

Karen Davis, Oklahoma City, Oklahoma—Tea-Smoked Ginger Sesame Burgers

Monty Degenhardt, Indianapolis, Indiana—Tuna, Mint, and Wheatberry Burgers with Three-Citrus Salsa

Margie Godwin, Greensboro, North Carolina—Stir-Fry Topped Burgers

Janet Hill, Sacramento, California—Golden Salmon Burgers

Carol Ann Islam, Corvallis, Oregon—Oriental Shrimp Burgers with Mushroom Relish Sauté

Judith Mettlin, Snyder, New York—Hunan Chicken Burgers

Julie Winter, Grosse Pointe Park, Michigan—Third-Coast Grilled Veal Burgers

1992

No contest

1993

Winners

Grand Prize: Robert Allen, Port Townsend, Washington—Gingered-Beef Burgers

First Prize: Diane Lentz, Nicholasville, Kentucky—Peppered Jamaican Jerk Burgers Normandy

Second Prize: Caryl Welsh, Clarksville, Maryland—Choucroute Burgers with Green Apple Salsa

Third Prize: Janet Steck, Cortland, New York—Tuscan Burgers Bruschetta

Award for Creativity: Robert Anzovino, San Jose, California—Beijing Burgers

Other Finalists*

Linda Ackerman—Blackberry Wine Burgers

Susan Asanovic, Wilton, Connecticut—Four-Chile Fiesta Burgers with Cool Tomatillo Salsa

Gloria Bradley, Naperville, Illinois—Greek Burgers with Tomato-Cucumber Relish

Karen Davis—Chorizo Burgers

Janice Elder, Charlotte, North Carolina—Smoked Salmon Burgers with Roasted Corn Salsa

Porter Lansing, Englewood, Colorado—Burgers DiMedici

Theodore Skiba, Tequesta, Florida—Green Peppercorn Duck Burgers

*The hometowns and states of two of the 1993 finalists are missing from Sutter Home's files. For the record, if you know that information, please contact BBB, Sutter Home Family Vineyards, P.O. Box 248, St. Helena, CA 94574.

1994

Winners

Grand Prize: Kurt Wait, Redwood City, California—Portobello Burgers

First Prize: Nancy Strande, Snohomish, Washington—Peppered Lamb Burgers with "Hot Tomato" Jam

Second Prize: Ellen Burr. Truro, Massachusetts—Brazilian Burgers

Award for Creativity: Janie Duffy, Dripping Springs, Texas—Tropical Burgers

Other Finalists

Eddy Jones, Okemos, Michigan—Grilled Hamburgers Au Poivre

Kathy Morikawa, Natural Bridge Station, Virginia—W-W Burgers

Theodore Skiba, Tequesta, Florida—Ginger Grouper Burgers with Mango Mustard

1995

Winners

Grand Prize: Porter Lansing, Englewood, Colorado—Chicken Oriental Burgers with Grilled Shiitake

First Prize: Vince Grosse, Marietta, Georgia—Mediterranean Tuna Burgers with Lemon-Basil Mayonnaise

Second Prize: Martin Kokotaylo, Sylvania, Ohio—Green Chile Chicken Burgers with Orange-Chili Mayonnaise and Three-Pepper Cheese Spread

Award for Creativity: Nicol Spedus, Petaluma, California—San Francisco Cioppino Burgers

Other Finalists

Gloria Bradley, Naperville, Illinois—Peppered Pita Burgers with Apple-Shallot Chutney

Lisa Keys, Middlebury, Connecticut—Greek Salad Burgers

Lloyd Roczniak, Rochester, Minnesota—Lamb Burgers with Minted Mango Chutney

1996

Winners

Grand Prize: Lori Welander, Shelburne, Vermont—Mulligatawny Burgers

First Prize: Lloyd Roczniak, Rochester, Minnesota—Fresh Salmon Burgers with Lemon-Cilantro Mayonnaise

Second Prize: Edwina Gadsby, Great Falls, Montana—Casablanca Burgers with Citrus-Olive Relish and Harissa Aioli

Award for Creativity: Julie Winter, Grosse Pointe Park, Michigan—Indian Burgers with Grilled Banana Raita

Other Finalists

Joyce Bowman, Raleigh, North Carolina—Bimbukuu Groundnut Burgers with Black Bean Salsa

Connie Emerson, Reno, Nevada—Casbah Burgers with Moroccan Mint Sauce

Paula McHargue, Richmond, Kentucky—Olympic Burgers with Georgia Peach Salsa

1997

Winners

Grand Prize: Susan Asanovic, Wilton, Connecticut—Siciliano Burgers with Fresh Ciliegine and Sweet Tomato Butter

First Prize: Mary Lou Newhouse, South Burlington, Vermont—Jamaican Me Crazy Burgers

Second Prize: Gloria Piantek, Skillman, New Jersey—Cubana Pork Burgers

Other Finalists

Gina Bolles, Marietta, Georgia—Homestead "Ham"burgers

David Conwell, Fairhope, Alabama—Hot Beefy-Dog Burgers with Sweet-Hot Mustard

Mark Forbert, Pacifica, California—South of the Border Burgers

Bob Gadsby, Great Falls, Montana—Black Thai Beef Burgers with Sautéed Shiitakes

Edie Young, San Francisco, California—Garlic-Grilled Thai Turkey Burgers

1998

Winners

Grand Prize: Larry Elder, Charlotte, North Carolina—Carolina Pork Barbecue Burgers

First Prize: Jason Boulanger, Williston, Vermont—Caesar Salad and Flank Steak Burgers with Garlic Crostini

Second Prize: Ron Perkins, Scottsdale, Arizona—Samurai Burgers

Award for Creativity: Debbie Vanni, Libertyville, Illinois—Sauerbraten Burgers

Other Finalists

Connie Emerson, Reno, Nevada—Burgers Italiano with Avocado Aioli

Richard McHargue, Richmond, Kentucky—Caribbean Couscous Burgers with Mango Salsa

Theodore Skiba, Tequesta, Florida—Stilton-Glazed Toasted Walnut Sirloin Burgers with Grilled Tomatoes and Spicy Leeks

1999

Winner

Grand Prize: Julie DeMatteo, Clementon, New Jersey—Down Island Burgers with Mango Mayo & Grilled Onions

Other Finalists

Frances Benthin, Scio, Oregon—Korean Beef Burgers with Creamy Kimchi Sauce

Wolfgang Hanau, West Palm Beach, Florida—Bertesca Piedmont Burgers with Gorgonzola and Grilled Italian Eggplant and Tomato Salad

Camilla Saulsbury, Bloomington, Indiana—Punjabi Burgers with Grilled Mango and Raita

Patricia Schroedl, Jefferson, Wisconsin—Belt-Bustin' Chile Burgers with Cheddar Cilantro Butter

2000

Winner

Grand Prize: Jamie Miller, Maple Grove, Minnesota—Hawaiian Tuna Burgers with Maui Wowee Salsa

Other Finalists

Steve Bradley, Bolingbrook, Illinois—Asiago Pine Nut Burgers with Smokey Aioli

Mary Louise Lever, Rome, Georgia—Shogun Char-Grilled Beef Burgers

Frank Rodriquez, Houston, Texas—Vintner's Burgers Provençal

Claudia Shepardson, Loudonville, New York—Roquefort Lamb Burgers with Grilled Pears

2001

Winners

Grand Prize: Kristine Snyder, Kihei, Hawaii—Soy-Glazed Salmon Burgers with Ginger-Lime Aioli

People's Choice Award: Norma Molitor, Austin, Texas—Tamarind-Glazed Thai Burgers

Other Finalists

Patti Honda Blezard, Honolulu, Hawaii—Tuscan Turkey Burgers

Joyce Bowman, Raleigh, North Carolina—Ranch-Hand Grilled Buffalo Burgers with Chipotle 'n' Honey Glaze and Corn 'n' Avocado Salsa

Norma Fried, Denver, Colorado—Pastrami BagelBurgers with Quick ZinfanDills

TerryAnn Moore, Oaklyn, New Jersey—Anytime Grilled Brunchburgers*

L. Monique Porche-Smith, Canton, Georgia—Bayou Burgers with Balsamic Spinach Slaw

Richard Rizzio, Traverse City, Michigan—Grilled Eggplant and Fennel Burgers with Tomato Tapenade

Claudia Shepardson, Loudonville, New York—Green Mountain Burgers*

Diane Sparrow, Osage, Iowa—Fruit of the Vine Burgers with California Relish

*Withdrew from the competition due to the events of September 11, 2001.

2002

Winners

Grand Prize (Best Beef Burger): Annelle Williams, Martinsville, Virginia—Vitello Focaccia

Best Alternative Burger: Kelly Bailer Krauss, Little Falls, New Jersey—Spicy Summer Shrimp Burgers with Crisp Pancetta

People's Choice Award: Adam Payson, Omaha, Nebraska—Chipotle-Honey BBQ Bacon Burgers with Gorgonzola Cheese

Other Finalists

Best Beef Burger

Scott Collier, Austin, Texas—Burgers Wellington

Karen Nicholes McVarish, Davis, California—Relleno Burgers with Fresh Chile–Mango Salsa

Susan Mello, Jackson Heights, New York—Portuguese Pineapple Picando Burgers

Best Alternative Burger

Virginia C. Anthony, Blowing Rock, North Carolina—Autumn Pork and Apple Burgers

Jim Bradley, Chicago, Illinois—Ragin' Cajun Pecan Pork Burgers with Spicy Onions

Robin Ekiss, San Francisco, California—Thanksgiving Turkey Burgers with Cranberry-Pecan-Mint Pesto

Peter Halferty, Corpus Christi, Texas—Peking Duck Burgers

2003

Winners

Grand Prize: Susan Mello, Jackson Heights, New York—My Big Fat Greco-Inspired Burgers

Best Professional Burger: Justin Ward, chef/owner, Harvest Restaurant, Atlanta, Georgia—Andouille-Shrimp Burgers with Creole Honey Mustard

People's Choice Award: Nikki Norman, Milton, Tennessee—Buttered Pecan Buffalo Burgers with Cabernet Cranberries and Herbed Mayonnaise

Best Potato Side Dish: Elaine Sweet, Dallas, Texas—Really Red Jackets with Tomato Chevre Gratin

Other Finalists

Build a Better Burger

Margee Berry, White Salmon, Washington—Noteworthy Northwest Burgers with Revved-Up Raspberry Ketchup

Loanne Chiu, Fort Worth, Texas—Indian Masala Burgers with Cucumber Raita

John Hanrahan, Winlock, Washington—Bahn Mi Burgers

Karyn Hentz, Arlington, Virginia—Kokomo Burgers

Daniel Howard, Lockport, Illinois—Guava Jack Burgers with Roasted Pepper and Avocado Salsa

Jay Kakuk, Plymouth, Minnesota—The Cobb

Mary Beth Harris Murphree, Tyler, Texas—3 Times the Garlic, 3 Times the Flavor Burgers!

Peter Thomas, West Hartford, Connecticut—3-2-1 Hamburgers

Professional Division

Harry Crane, executive chef, Kraft Foodservice, Glenview, Illinois—Manchego Melt with Chipotle-Avocado Aioli

Craig Priebe, executive chef, Henry Crown and Company, Glen Ellyn, Illinois—Double Blue Berry Burgers

Fred Ramos, Printer's Row Restaurant, Chicago, Illinois—Venison Burgers with Tabasco-Chipotle Mayonnaise

Howie Velie, C.E.C., Charlottesville, Virginia—Grilled Buffalo Chicken Burgers with Fresh Bleu Cheese Dressing on a Cornduster Kaiser

Potato Side Dish

Liz Barclay, Annapolis, Maryland—Hot Potato Tort

Lillian Julow, Gainesville, Florida—Baker's Potato Pie

Carole Resnick, Cleveland, Ohio—Mushroom, Artichoke, Roasted Pepper, and Olive Tart in a Crispy Potato Crust

Douglas Root, Kennewick, Washington—Chipotle Potato Salad

2004

Winner

Grand Prize: Clint Stephenson, Friendswood, Texas—Grilled California Avocado BLT Burgers with Caramelized Chipotle Onions

Other Finalists

Debbi Bracker, Carl Junction, Missouri—Peppercorn Burgers with Goat Cheese Spread & Honeyed Greens

Veronica Callaghan, Glastonbury, Connecticut—All-American Hero Burgers with Avocado-Tomato Dressing

Jan Curry, Raleigh, North Carolina—Midway Hamburger Steak Sandwiches

Jenny Flake, Gilbert, Arizona—Feta Sun-Dried Tomato Stuffed Prosciutto Burgers

Christopher Kirigin, New York, New York—All-American Zinburgers

Nikki Norman, Winter Park, Florida—Island-Style Key West Burgers with Caribbean Mayonnaise

Darlya Oehler, Ingram, Texas—Colibri Ranch's Mesquite-Grilled Centennial Burgers

Karen Tedesco, Webster Groves, Missouri—New-Fashioned American Drive-In Cheeseburgers

Tom Wickham, Portland, Oregon—Southwest "Chili" Burgers with Avocado Crema and Lime-Marinated Slaw

Recipe Index

Photo Credits

page iii: Getty Images
page 3 (right): Andrew Rice
page 6 (bottom right): Valdine Chirico
page 8 (top center): Andrew Moore
page 9 (top right): Andrew Rice
page 10: M. J. Wickham
page 11 (center): Valdine Chirico
page 12 (top): Tombrock Corporation, White Tower, Camden #8 (1955)
page 13 (top): Corbis
page 13 (bottom): Richard Hailey, Texas Pig Stands
page 14 (top): The Huntington Library, San Marino, California, from the "Dick" Whittington Collection
page 14 (bottom): Corbis
page 15 (top): University of Louisville Photographic Archives, Caufield and Shook Collection
page 15 (bottom): Corbis
page 16: Ronald L. McDonald, reprinted with the permission of the author from *Ronald McDonald's International Burger Book.*
page 18: Ronald L. McDonald, reprinted with the permission of the author from *Ronald McDonald's International Burger Book.*
page 30: Andrew Moore
page 31: Valdine Chirico
page 42: Robert Holmes
page 43: Peter Allen
page 55: Robert Holmes
page 56: M. J. Wickham
page 57: Virginia Wait
page 66: Robert Holmes
page 78: M. J. Wickham
page 79: Andrew Moore
page 88: Andrew Rice
page 89: Andrew Rice
page 96: Andrew Moore
page 106: Robert Holmes
page 110: Robert Holmes
page 120: Robert Holmes
page 128: M. J. Wickham
page 141: Robert Holmes
page 142: Corbis
page 144 (top left): Andrew Moore
page 147: Andrew Rice
page 149: Andrew Moore
page 167: M. J. Wickham
page 180: Kansas State Historical Society
page 185 (top left): Andrew Rice
page 188 (right): Dan Mills
page 189: M. J. Wickham
page 191: Robert Holmes
page 192: Tristin Chirico (Robert Chirico); Monte Nuss (Porter Lansing); Sean Busher (Larry Elder); Steve Strand (Kristine Snyder); Ann Simmons (Susan Mello); M. J. Wickham (Clint Stephenson)
page 193: Andrew Moore
page 201: M. J. Wickham